Instructor's Manual
and
Test Bank to Accompany

School & Society
Educational Practice as Social Expression

STEVEN E. TOZER
University of Illinois
Urbana–Champaign

PAUL C. VIOLAS
University of Illinois
Urbana–Champaign

GUY B. SENESE
Northern Illinois University

JEAN BUTTRIDGE
University of Illinois
Urbana–Champaign

McGraw-Hill, Inc.
New York   St. Louis   San Francisco   Auckland   Bogotá
Caracas   Lisbon   London   Madrid   Mexico   Milan
Montreal   New Delhi   San Juan   Singapore
Sydney   Tokyo   Toronto

INSTRUCTOR'S MANUAL to accompany

School & Society: Educational Practice as Social Expression

Acknowledgements

We wish to express our appreciation to Lane Akers, who developed the overall concept of this manual, and to Rupert Berk and David Rein, who contributed suggestions based on their experience teaching from a draft of the text. We also take this opportunity to thank Huey Li Li, who provided valuable assistance in the writing of the textbook itself.

Jean Bettridge, Steven Tozer, Paul Violas, and Guy Senese

CONTENTS

Introduction

Using *School and Society*

Throughout the United States, courses in social foundations of education are characterized by an interesting paradox: they are, together with courses in psychological foundations of education, among the courses most often mandated by state boards of education for teacher education programs, but they are at the same time the most often criticized by students as being least interesting and least important for their professional preparation. Criticism of courses in foundational disciplines such as history, philosophy, sociology, and anthropology of education, together with criticism of the distinctively cross-disciplinary approach known since the late 1930s as social foundations of education, is levelled not just by students, but by scholars as well. From James B. Conant in the 1960s to Sirotnik and Goodlad in the 1990s, those who have studied teacher preparation programs have raised challenges to social foundations educators about the value and efficacy of our work.

While such criticism is widespread, it is not uniform. Social foundations educators who gather at the annual conference of the American Educational Studies Association report high levels of student and faculty satisfaction with social foundations courses in various large and small institutions throughout the country--and we faculty learn from one another's successes. The textbook that this manual is designed to accompany is based on one of those courses--Educational Policy Studies 201, which has been taught successfully at the University of Illinois Urbana-Champaign for seventeen years. It has consistently received outstanding student ratings, and the faculty and teaching assistants who have taught this course have received a variety of College and campus-wide teaching honors for their work. Our purpose in designing this manual is to preserve key dimensions of what has made the course successful over the years, while recognizing that *School and Society: Educational Practice as Social Expression* will be used by faculty who are specialists in social foundations as well as faculty whose specializations lie outside the foundational disciplines.

THE TWO-PART STRUCTURE

The approach to social foundations of education instruction that has guided this text is based on the historical development of that field at Teacher's College Columbia and later at the University of Illinois Urbana-Champaign.   This approach distinguishes its coursework from coursework in "introduction to education courses" by emphasizing that social foundations coursework expressly seeks to engage students in a critical, integrated, cross-disciplinary analysis of social institutions, processes, and ideals that equips educators to make informed, normative judgments about the relations between school and society. [1] Historically, introduction to education courses have no such critical, cross-disciplinary, integrated tradition. Our commitment to this tradition lies partly in our respect for the way in which our predecessors originally conceived the field and its contribution to the preparation of educators. We believe the problems that teachers confront in their daily practice are multidimensional, and that study of the historical, sociological, philosophical, and other cultural dimensions of these problems will better equip teachers to interpret and respond to them.

To achieve this integrated, cross-disciplinary approach, we have developed a two-part structure to School and Society. Part 1 is historical, engaging students in critical analysis of key developments in the origins of modern schooling from Colonial times to the post-Sputnik reform era. Part 2 engages students in critical analysis of such contemporary educational issues as ideology, race, ethnicity, gender, social class, and the control of schooling by recalling those same issues in Part 1. Thus, each chapter in Part 2 has at least one corresponding historical chapter in Part 1.   In contrast to social foundations texts that present individual chapters on philosophy of education, sociology of education, history of education, control of schooling, multicultural education, and so on, these issues are integrated cumulatively throughout this text. Each chapter successively builds on all the chapters that come before it.

Students are encouraged to critique the policies and practices of historical and contemporary educators, using the analysis presented by the authors of the text, and reading critically, with newly informed perspectives, the primary source readings at the end

---

1. See, for example, the discussion of this approach in *Tozer, Steven and Stuart McAninch.   "Social Foundations of Education in Historical Perspective." *Educational Foundations*, Vol. 1, No. 1, Fall 1986, pp. 5-32.

of each chapter. By evaluating the ideas expressed in the primary source readings, students will see that not everyone in a given historical era saw the world in exactly the same way. Most of the primary source readings show individuals who are critical of the major educators portrayed in the chapter narratives, and students should be helped to see that, while educators' ideas are influenced by their historical conditions, they are not *determined* by those conditions, and that today's educators--our students included--have a responsibility to make evaluative judgments for themselves about dominant trends in educational practice. This opportunity, to form and to have defend their own evaluative judgments with historical, philosophical, and sociological insights, is a major component of what students value in our social foundations course over the years.

THE ROLE OF STRUCTURED DIALOGUE IN TEACHING *SCHOOL AND SOCIETY*

What has made the course a valued learning experience for the students, faculty, and teaching assistants who participate in it? The answer lies in the fact that only part of the course content can be reproduced in a textbook; the other, equally important, part is generated by students and faculty in dialogue stimulated by what they read.

It is our view that the most effective use of *School and Society* requires engaging students in a systematic, critical analysis of historical, sociological, and ideological dimensions of an institution with which they are familiar, giving them a personal and intellectual relationship with scholarly perspectives they might otherwise find abstract and dead. By engaging the students in a *critical* analysis, the book challenges a number of perspectives on schooling and society that students have learned to take for granted. For example, the view that "ability grouping" serves the interests of some students at the expense of others--often moves many preservice teachers to defend their own long-established views against the critical views of the book. Discussions of how schooling can exacerbate gender and race discrimination allows students who have felt such discrimination find voice through an account more systematic and critical than they previously have encountered in their school.

But what of the *integration* of that critical content with course processes? Here the pedagogy employed in using *School and Society* becomes a central issue. This volume (like any, we would argue, but perhaps more so when students' world views are being challenged) demands an opportunity for oral and written dialogue among students and among students and faculty. The content of *School and Society* is not intended to be taught as facts and analyses to be learned and recited as the "truth" about school and society, but rather shows perspectives that students can understand and evaluate for the consequences those perspectives have for the students' own thinking about the sociopolitical and educational world around them. On the other hand, our emphasis on student dialogue should not be misunderstood as the view that the text is useful only as a stimulus to discussion--as if the textbook content is less important than the process of students talking about their own experiences. We do not value, in our own teaching, talk for talk's sake, and we believe the analysis presented in various ways throughout this volume is important for the prospective teacher to understand and evaluate.

Students are expected to *understand* the analysis presented in this volume, for without that understanding they will not be able to evaluate that analysis, nor to test their prior understandings against it, nor to incorporate dimensions of that analysis intelligently and critically into their own thinking. But understanding is an act of interpretation, of meaning-construction, and students should be helped to understand that the textbook itself is a network of constructed meanings or interpretations that are subject to criticism, evaluation, and reinterpretation. *It is our experience that most students cannot be expected to engage in rich meaning-construction using the concepts of this volume simply by reading it,* any more than they could learn to play a musical instrument well by reading an instruction booklet alone. Just as learning to play the instrument requires hands-on activity, so learning to construct meaning well, using new concepts, requires active practice in using them. Classroom dialogue and opportunities to evaluate these textbook ideas in writing provide just such practice, and students can become fluent in a new vocabulary of analysis if they are given sufficient interactive opportunities. Thus, this Instructor's Manual seeks to promote student dialogue, both oral and written. Students are encouraged to critique their own arguments seriously to see if they might improve their ability to form, articulate, evaluate and defend their beliefs. It is our view that good teachers must be good thinkers, adept at constructing meaning, taking positions on the basis of interpretation formed, and providing reasons for those positions.

In keeping with the questions for discussion and examination at the end of each chapter in *School and Society,* this Instructor's Manual focuses on discussion and essay questions that have a common conceptual structure: students are asked to take a position on some socio-educational problem and then defend their position with the use of evidence and argument. To assist faculty in providing occasions for students to engage in such practice, the Manual presents each chapter divided into five general dimensions: Chapter Objectives, Chapter Overview, Teaching Suggestions, Essay Questions, and Multiple-Choice Questions. Prior to examining these five components of each chapter of the Instructor's Manual, however, it is useful to take a closer look at the kind of structured classroom dialogue we have in mind.

CLASSROOM DIALOGUE: ASKING "THE GOOD QUESTION"

The four most easily identifiable components of a course that uses *School and Society* are the textbook (and perhaps supplemental) readings; instructor-presented material such as lectures and films; classroom discussion; and written assignments. Some foundations courses may also include field placements. Of these components, classroom discussion is probably the most complex.

The unique potential of discussion sessions lies in what they can accomplish that no other component of a course can: guided discussion and debate **among students** about the social and educational issues raised in the text. Such discussion is not valuable for the sake of conversation, but instead for the achievement of understanding that emerges through the use of course concepts.

UNDERSTANDING THROUGH PARTICIPATION

The essential content of *School and Society* can best be generated through a dialogical process. Employing this process assumes, first, that most students have attended to the content of any instructor-presented material such as lectures, even though they may not thoroughly understand it. Second, it assumes that some students--rarely all of them--have done most of the reading and understood some of it. Third, it assumes that students bring to class a wealth of experience, understanding, and interests that are **directly relevant** to the content of each chapter and original source reading. Finally, it assumes that faculty can build on this substantial but inadequate base by identifying **for themselves** why this particular reading is important and by directing attention quickly to those issues. *In doing so, the important task for the faculty member is to formulate a problem that is engaging for the students because it bridges text content and students' prior* *experiences--a problem that will draw them into the activity of discussion so that understanding may follow.*

Consider the following analogies. The first is a baseball game in which only the coach knows the rules and everyone else is relatively new to the game. The coach does not require anyone to know the rules before allowing them to participate. The coach shows the players what to do in a brief and general way and then starts the game. As they participate, the players gain an understanding of the rules, as well as other dimensions of the conceptual "content" of baseball. They may not know the rules after the first game, but after a few games, a substantial understanding of the rules emerges. Meaning is constructed through participation.

Now imagine, instead, if the coach had to make sure everyone understood the "content" of baseball before they were allowed to play. Everyone would take much longer to get on the field; some would never get there; the understandings held by all participants would be distorted by being removed from actual practice

A second analogy familiar to many is playing "Go Fish" with pre-schoolers who cannot yet read many of the numbers. The adult must guide the game as it proceeds, making sure that numbers are not mis-read, etc., but at no point does the adult make an effort to teach the numbers as a separate or pre-requisite body of knowledge. Yet soon all the children know their numbers as well as the rules and strategy of the game. The numbers were conceptual tools they acquired in service of the business at hand, namely, the game. They were not motivated to learn numbers, **per se**, but were motivated to participate in the game. Again, meaning has emerged through use.

These analogies are not meant to be applied too literally; there are conceptual differences between them--and between such games and leading a discussion. What is interesting here are the similarities, in which students are motivated to participate in an activity for its own sake--in the case at hand, a discussion of some problem that touches them--and in doing so, they develop new understandings that bring them proficiently into a new community of dialogue.

On this model, one does not seek to establish the essential content of a paper, chapter, or lecture before the discussion develops. The content emerges--less systematically, but more meaningfully for the students--**through** the discussion. The teacher's task is to provide a context--a problem that both you and the students find worthy of discussion--to bring that content to life.

TECHNIQUE: DIFFERENT KINDS OF QUESTIONS

Notice which of the following ways of posing a question is most likely to generate interest and discussion:

1. What does Van Doren (Chapter 7) say about similarities between humans?

2. Van Doren says people are generally similar in their intellectual nature, so all people should be educated the same. Based on your own experience, do you believe that?

One of the essential differences between these questions is that with one of them you can call on any student in the room and expect some kind of an answer; an answer to which other students can respond, based on their own understandings and experiences. The other question is one you would expect most students in the room would meet with silence if you called on them individually; because they have not read the material, because they simply missed that point, or because they were not confident their answer was the "right" answer.

The other advantage of such a question as the second (and it is not really a very imaginative or provocative one, compared to many that you might use) is that it allows you to involve most all the students, not just those who have "done their homework." People do not learn to use tools, manual or conceptual, well just by watching others use them--they must get some experience themselves. Some ways of asking questions, and conducting a class in general, encourage everyone to use conceptual tools actively, while other ways encourage only a few students to use them. And the conceptual tools that students are learning to use should be grounded in *School and Society*: new vocabulary, new insights into political economy, ideology, and schooling, new ways of thinking historically and sociologically, and so on. If the discussion questions are framed appropriately, bridges are built between student perceptions of their own experiences and the essential content of the book. Each chapter ends with samples of such questions, and others are included in this manual. The instructor is encouraged to develop more, based on his or her superior knowledge of the students, their environment, and their prior experiences.

A NOTE ON TRADITIONS OF AUTHORITY BETWEEN TEACHER AND STUDENT

The nature of the traditional classroom, in which the teacher faces the class from behind a desk or podium, is often *authoritarian*, as opposed to an exercise of authority consistent with democratic ideals, which might be termed *authoritative*. In authoritarian classrooms, a teacher wields authority so that students have neither the opportunity nor the expectation of influencing the conduct and processes of the classroom. Insofar as faculty replicate that traditional classroom configuration and its social relations, they (we) help set up traditional classroom expectations, in which the students see themselves more as recorders of information than as participants in generating understanding.

These authority issues are importantly connected to the kinds of questions raised in discussions. We can assume that most students arrive at college with years of experience in producing "the right answer" for their teachers, and this creates a set of expectations easy for the instructor to fall into. Asking questions that have a right answer (e.g., "What is Jefferson's position on local control of schooling?") will elicit traditional "studenting" responses.

Students are quite familiar with such traditional teaching questions and correctly perceive the teacher's stance to be, "I know the answer and I'm testing to see if you know." While this may be legitimate at times, it should not be confused with a discussion. While some students are disposed to cooperating with such a traditional mode of questioning, many have long ago developed a stance of merely tolerating such questions, and even very good students often develop something like resistance to them: "If called on, I'll participate, but not otherwise." Nowhere else in our social lives do we ask people questions to which we already know the answers, and this artificiality pervades and stifles the classroom interaction when this is the kind of question primarily relied on by faculty.

If the students perceive the point of a question not to be a test of their knowledge, but as a legitimate effort to investigate a problem, their response is generally dramatically different. When faculty adopt an investigatory posture, students are typically eager to assist in the investigation. Even resistant or apathetic-appearing students quickly warm to such tasks as criticizing claims made in the textbook that do not seem confirmed in their own experience, clearing up a genuine ambiguity, or informing the instructor of something he or she needs to know about student experiences in order to proceed.

The contrast being drawn here is not formal vs. informal atmosphere, personable vs. remote style, or "open-ended" vs. closed questions. It has more to do with the apparent motive of the instructor: investigating an issue vs. teaching a body of concepts. *Student participation in the former is a uniquely valuable way of achieving the latter.*

The problem of *pretending* to investigate is a serious one, however. If perceived as pretending to investigate a matter on which his or her mind is already made up, the teacher is seen to be using a teaching technique, and the students assume habituated roles which might be called "student technique." The teacher needs to decide in advance of each class what genuinely needs investigating and what students can contribute to that. Therefore, the investigation to be conducted should be incomplete without students' reports and reflection upon their own experience.

COMPONENTS OF EACH CHAPTER OF THE INSTRUCTOR'S MANUAL

Chapter Objectives
The purpose of providing a brief list of some of the major objectives of each chapter is to help the teacher decide what portions of the chapter to emphasize, orient the teacher to the purposes of the discussion and exam questions at the end of each chapter, and help the teacher make judgments about the wide range of possible classroom activities and discussion topics in terms of *presenting* students with a particular analysis or illustration for their consideration; or in terms of helping students *deepen and extend* their thinking on a particular issue, or in terms of having students think critically about or analyze a particular set of phenomena or analysis of these phenomena. The chapter objectives remind the professor that the objective is not primarily to have students learn that something is true, but rather to have students engage in particular kinds of thinking about social and educational policies, practices, and ideas: thinking that is informed by scholarship in the relevant disciplines; thinking that is critically analytic and evaluative.

Chapter Overview

The chapter overview presents a one- or two-paragraph abstract of the chapter content. It summarizes the general narrative flow of the chapter and alerts the teacher to the major issues addressed therein. In addition, each chapter of the textbook itself ends with a section, "Concluding Remarks," that offers summary and reflection on major themes presented in the chapter.

Teaching Suggestions

We have included this section in each chapter simply as a place to pass along the benefit of some of our own experiences in teaching these materials. We hope to expand this section as we hear from faculty who find their own ways to use *School and Society* innovatively and effectively. In particular, we use this section to suggest why particular primary source readings were selected and what they offer to the student.

Essay Questions: Short-Answer and Full Essay

These are self-explanatory in each chapter and can be used, like the questions at the end of each of chapter of the text, for discussion, examination, or written assignments. All require students to take a position on some issue and to defend that position with evidence and argument.

Multiple-Choice Questions (A Cautionary Note)

There are teachers at all levels, elementary school through graduate school, who refuse to use multiple-choice questions in their teaching and student evaluation. In our own teaching at the undergraduate and graduate levels, for example, we forego multiple-choice questions entirely in favor of two- to ten-page essay assignments. We find several problems with multiple-choice questions:

- they tend to reward and stimulate literal recall of text material rather than stimulating more complex analytical thought;

- they tend to reward students for replicating or recognizing the limited number of conceptual relationships among facts and ideas the test authors have written into the questions, rather than for creatively constructing conceptual relationships of their own;

- they tend to be less challenging and intellectually demanding for students in that they do not require students to express their ideas in effective prose but instead reward students for being able to select a single pre-authored phrase or sentence from among several such phrases in sentences;

- they do not allow for the kind of diagnoses of student understandings, and subsequent dialogue with students over their constructed meanings, that are facilitated by evaluating and responding to students' written prose.

Moreover, the characterization of multiple-choice questions as "objective," while essay questions are portrayed as "subjective," is fundamentally misleading about the nature of knowledge itself. One could plausibly argue that multiple-choice tests are much more "subjective" since they require students to match the thought processes of a particular test author, while essay tests are more "objective" because they do not impose the test author's subjective view of the "right answer" on the student, but rather allow the student's meaning-construction to be tested according to widely-accepted criteria of valid use of evidence and argument.

However . . .

Despite these and other limitations of multiple-choice questions, we recognize that some faculty members may base their choice of whether or not to use this textbook on the availability of such questions. In many cases there are good reasons for this choice: faculty who are required to teach unreasonably heavy loads of students may find that in their circumstances, the opportunity to respond adequately to student essays is a luxury they cannot afford. Therefore, we have sought to construct essay questions that do not easily fall into the tendencies identified above. They reward and stimulate inferential understandings, for example, rather than literal recall. They are constructed to avoid focus on discrete facts in favor of focus on more complex relationships among ideas. Some faculty will still find these questions unnecessary to accomplish their purposes, even antithetical to them, while others will find them useful for evaluating students' basic understanding of the textbook narrative in each chapter. We would urge all faculty, however, to find ways to challenge students with the more demanding essay questions, either in classroom discussion or in written essays or, preferably, both.

Chapter 1

Understanding School and Society

CHAPTER OBJECTIVES

Among the objectives that Chapter 1 seeks to achieve are these:

1. Students should become acquainted with basic conceptual tools to be used throughout the book, especially political economy, ideology, and schooling, which are said to have interactive influence on one another, though that influence will not be of equal proportion.

2. By entertaining the view that the best theory explains practical phenomena and can therefore guide practice, students should reflect critically on the cliched view that "theory" and "practice" are opposed to one another.

3. Students should consider basic distinctions among schooling, training, and education so they can begin to reflect on the concept of education as a value-laden ideal that allows them to evaluate schooling and training practices for their educational worth.

4. Students are intended to consider the Feudal European and Classical Athenian periods as occasions for interpreting relationships among the political-economy, ideology, and schooling practices of each illustration. The objective here is to familiarize students with how these basic tools of inquiry work in practice by giving the students practice in using them on specific cases on which they have limited information.

5. Students are to begin considering the meanings and limitations of the concept "democracy" in cultural context, with sensitivity toward the egalitarian impulses of a society that would select its legislators by lot and with sensitivity as well toward how a "democratic" culture can exclude most of its residents from political participation.

CHAPTER OVERVIEW

Chapter 1 introduces students to the basic analytic vocabulary, or "tools of inquiry," used throughout *School and Society*, with an emphasis on why social theory is important to consider if we intend to understand schooling. The common opposition of the "theoretical" and the "practical" is challenged on the grounds that good social theory seeks to identify and explain actual phenomena, including phenomena of practice. It also describes the three-part analytic framework used throughout the book, in which the terms political economy, ideology, and schooling are understood as interactively influencing one another, rather than a more uni-directional model in which, for example, the economic base determines all educational practices. Finally, brief sketches of Feudal Europe and Classical Athens are presented so that students will be able to see how these three analytic components might be used to understand and interpret the relations between culture and schooling.

TEACHING SUGGESTIONS

Students should be engaged as soon as possible in critical discussion involving the major terms of Chapter 1. Instructors are encouraged to use the structured dialogue approach described in the Instructor's Manual *Introduction*. The end-of-chapter questions might prove useful in this regard.

One means of getting students quickly engaged in discussing ideas in a large-group setting is to pass out notecards and ask for a written response to a question of the instructor's choice, then collect and redistribute the cards so that no student has his or her own. Students feel freer to read the response of an anonymous "other" than to risk their own ideas so early in a course. As student responses are read, other students can be encouraged to critically appraise these responses and a tone of respectful criticism of ideas can be established with any students having taken personal risks.

It is our experience that students have difficulty understanding the concept of ideology, especially early in the course when they have not discussed how ideology operates in concrete historical contexts. They often think of ideology only as consciously held views that can be stated as articles of belief, for example, the belief that "all men are created equal." Students need to be helped to see that behind such belief-statements are a range of less-consciously articulated assumptions, values, and habits of thought that condition the meanings of such statements as "all men are created equal," and that an understanding of ideology helps us understand what words themselves mean for different actors in different historical settings. It cannot be expected that students will be well-versed in their understanding of the concepts of ideology and political economy, and the relations of these dimensions of culture to schooling, until later in the text when students have greater opportunity to use these concepts in their own discussion and writing.

ESSAY QUESTIONS

Below are two kinds of essay questions:

a. short essays or identification questions in which students are asked to write a descriptive paragraph or two to demonstrate their understanding of certain concepts, events, or practices; and

b. longer essays, which allow students to demonstrate their ability to analyze more complex issues involving several events, concepts, and/or practices.

A. Identify and briefly indicate the significance of an assigned number of the following:

a. schooling vs. education
b. political economy
c. ideology
d. the practicality of social theory
e. Athenian citizenship
f. Athenian slavery
g. "liberal studies"

B. Write a well-ordered essay, 2-3 pages in length, in response to an assigned number of questions from pages 11-12 of your text and from the two choices below. Your essay requires you to take a position on a socio-educational issue and then defend that position with reasoned argument and evidence from the text and from other sources at your disposal. In each essay, you are expected to:

   a. clearly state your position or thesis;
   b. respond to *all parts* of the assigned question;
   c. defend your position with evidence and reasoned argument;
   d. demonstrate college-level writing skills.

For each chapter of the text, a set of essay questions will be presented in the manual in addition to the set presented in the text itself. Both sets are intended to accomplish the same purposes and may be used interchangeably for discussion, assignments, and exams. Three questions are suggested for this chapter in addition to those in the text:

   1. Identify any classroom experience you can recall from your elementary or secondary education years and indicate whether that experience was primarily a case of schooling, training, or education--or some combination of these. Explain your assessment.

   2. Identify any practice in school that you think reflects some component of the prevailing belief-system, or ideology, of contemporary culture, and identify how the prevailing ideology might be used both to explain and to justify the schooling practice you have chosen. In your view, how adequate is that justification? Explain your position.

   3. Identify any prominent schooling practice--curricular or extra-curricular--that most American students have experienced, and explain how that practice contributes to preparing students for the political economy of the United States.

MULTIPLE-CHOICE ITEMS

For each item, select the *best* answer from the four alternatives presented, as supported by your textbook. Students are encouraged to defend answers other than those in the answer key with evidence and argument, which may or may not prove compelling enough to have an alternate answer counted as correct.

1. Social theory is an important analytical tool because it
    a. shows the differences between abstract ideas and practical reality
    b. leads to discovery of the truth of a phenomenon
    c. contributes to interpretive understanding of how or why something occurs
    d. all of the above

2. Schooling involves
    a. planned instruction and programs of study
    b. learning achieved through the hidden curriculum
    c. the state's goals for its citizens
    d. all of the above

3. Training differs from education in that training
    a. has no value to one's individuality
    b. attempts to get people to perform specific tasks in predictable manners
    c. is always used for achieving social control
    d. all of the above

4. Education has as an important goal
    a. one's self-creation
    b   one's ability to consider possible alternatives
    c. unanticipated responses to situations
    d. all of the above

5. Political economy most accurately refers to
    a. the political system of a society
    b. the economic stratification of a society
    c. the overall organization of a society
    d. all of the above

6. Ideology is a concept that includes
    a. the structure of a society's economic and governmental institutions
    b. a distortion of perspective on the part of those people holding the ideology
    c. how groups understand the organization of their society and others'
    d. all of the above

7. If you are able to describe the dominant ideology of your society, you
    a. have overcome its effects on your own analytical ability
    b. can easily identify the people who are blinded by it
    c. are better able to evaluate it
    d. all of the above

8. This book emphasizes certain analytical tools with the goal of
    a. helping students develop their abilities to critique their own society
    b. helping students to be better able to understand someone else's values
    c. helping students examine contemporary issues facing public schooling
    d. all of the above

9. The feudal belief in the divine right of kings is an example of
    a. prevailing religious doctrine during the feudal era
    b. the feudal hierarchy of education
    c. a component of an ideology
    d. all of the above

10. Systematic exclusion of some groups of people from the decision-making processes
    of their society occurs in societies considered to be
    a. democratic
    b. socialist
    c. communist
    d. all of the above

11. Athenian citizens were confident that manual labor would be performed by slaves and
    non-citizens primarily because
    a. their warlike society frequently enslaved vanquished soldiers
    b. the dominant ideology supported such a hierarchical division of labor and rights
    c. everyone believed that slaves were supposed to be manual laborers
    d. all of the above

12. The differences between the educational arrangements made for Athenian male citizens, females, and non-citizens are attributable to which of the following?

    a. an ideological commitment to the importance of leisure for, and the superior capacities of, free men

    b. the view that wealth should be a primary determinant of educational opportunity

    c. a strong commitment to the vocational value of education

    d. all of the above

13. Which of these might be said to emphasize a conformist model of citizenship more than independent thought?

    a. a teacher eliminates recess period until the people who drew graffiti on the blackboards come forward

    b. the school board establishes a policy that students may not stage a protest march on school grounds

    c. a student who has been warned several times about being disruptive is sent out of the classroom for the remainder of the day

    d. all of the above

14. The analytic framework presented in this chapter suggests that schooling policies are

    a. directly caused by changes in the political economy

    b. a product of a society's political-economic and ideological forces

    c. generally a primary cause of any society's ideological commitments

    d. all of the above

15. Busing students from one neighborhood to another to achieve racial balance in schools is evidence of the operation of

    a. ideology

    b. political economy

    c. schooling

    d. all of the above

Answer Key

1. C	2. D	3. B	4. D	5. C
6. C	7. C	8. D	9. C	10. D
11. B	12. A	13. D	14. B	15. B

Chapter 2

Liberty and Literacy: The Jeffersonian Ideal

CHAPTER OBJECTIVES

Among the objectives sought in Chapter 2 are these:

1. Students should deepen and extend their understanding of the key terms of inquiry, particularly the triad of political economy, ideology, and schooling, by seeing them applied in a particular historical context. In particular, students should be able to talk and write about the relationships among various dimensions of the political economy, ideology, and the nature of schooling in the early Republic.

2. Students should begin to critically evaluate the strengths and weaknesses of Classical Liberalism, noting its potential for realization of democratic ideals but noting also its limitations in terms of population groups excluded due to race, gender, and economic class.

3. Students should be able to understand Jefferson's rationale for his educational proposals as that rationale relates to the political economy and the ideology of that time.

4. Students should begin to entertain and evaluate alternative views of democracy: that it can be construed as a system of representative government, but also as an ideal of human interaction in which all individuals are expected to share in making the decisions that effect their lives. Further, they should begin thinking about the implications that each view of democracy might have for educational practices.

5. Students can be thinking about whether there might be potential for conflict between ideals of meritocracy and ideals of democracy, particularly if the definition of "merit" becomes the province of a some segment of the population that is not representative of the entire population.

6. Students should engage in thinking critically and appreciatively about Jefferson's proposals for who should fund and control public schooling in Virginia, comparing those ideas with how schooling is funded and controlled today.

CHAPTER OVERVIEW

Chapter 2 treats political economy, ideology, and schooling in the fifty years after the American Revolution. Chief features of the political economy of the early republic include an agrarian economy, decentralized republican government, relative homogeneity of local culture, and a social hierarchy importantly defined by race and gender. Ideologically, the origins of democratic thought in early America can be understood in the context of the breakdown of feudalism in Europe and the rise of classical liberalism in Europe and the United States. Each of the following features of classical liberalism helps define the character of the ideology shared by Jefferson and his contemporaries: a commitment to human reason, a belief in a universe governed by natural law, a conception of human virtue shaped by sacred and secular influences, a belief in the inevitability of progress, a growing sense of nationalism, and, finally, a multidimensional conception of freedom, the facets of which are detailed in the chapter itself.

The classic liberal commitment to education--and for Jefferson, free public education--can be understood in relationship to each of the components of classical liberalism identified above. To examine Thomas Jefferson's beliefs about popular schooling requires an understanding of Jefferson's views about the relationship between participatory democracy and education. In addition, his conception of mind and learning theory were grounded in "faculty psychology," which compared the mind in part to a muscle and in part to an empty vessel. Therefore, for Jefferson, formal education needed to be both broad and rigorous to sufficiently *exercise* the faculties of the mind and to *fill* it with the best of human learning.

One can rightly criticize Jefferson's racist and sexist assumptions, but in doing so, it is important to recognize that those assumptions were part and parcel of the limitations on classical liberal commitments to such ideals as reason, freedom, and democracy. The limitations of the dominant ideology are identified not to excuse Jefferson from his own biases, but to show the extent to which the meanings of such terms as "equality," "freedom," "education," and "virtue," vary with historical context.

TEACHING SUGGESTIONS

1. As students begin to think critically about the limitations of classical liberal ideology, they have a tendency to vilify, or at least to place at some distance from themselves, an ideology that by today's standards had significant racist and sexist dimensions. This tendency to distance themselves from the dominant ideology can also be seen among students as they later critique modern liberal ideology. The danger of this tendency is that the dominant ideology of our culture, and its historical origins, becomes externalized for students, as if they themselves have not been importantly shaped by it. While the students learn to critique the exclusionist tendencies of classical liberalism, they can also learn to identify and become more critical about their own thinking has been conditioned by classical liberal commitments to such ideals as objective truth, private property, and a view of democracy that represents some portions of the population but not others.

2. Students may have a tendency to wonder "what all this political economy and ideology has to do with being a teacher." Such a question should be anticipated and discussed in this chapter and in subsequent chapters. Students need to be helped, at first, to see the connections between cultural analysis and educational policies and practices.

3. The Benjamin Rush selection at chapter's end can serve to underscore for students the primary role that religion played in the thinking of many classical liberals prior to the establishment of strong traditions of separation of church and state in educational matters. They should be asked to look for evidence of classical liberal precepts in Rush, but also to see ways in which Rush and Jefferson differ--for example, in their approaches to intellectual freedom. Students can thus consider how individuals can share a common ideology yet differ in important elements of their beliefs and values.

ESSAY QUESTIONS

Below are two kinds of essay questions:

    a. short essays or identification questions in which students are asked to write a descriptive paragraph or two to demonstrate their interpretive understanding of certain concepts, events, or practices; and

      b. longer essays, which allow students to demonstrate their ability to analyze more complex issues involving several events, concepts, and/or practices.

A. Identify and briefly indicate the historical and educational significance of an assigned number of the following:

      a. Classical Liberalism

      b. Faculty Psychology

      c. Feudalism

      d. Natural Law

      e. Separation of Church and State

      f. Jeffersonian Realism

      g. "Natural Aristocracy"

      h. meritocracy

      i. Benjamin Rush

      j. Sir Isaac Newton

      k. "divine right"

      l. "Bill for the More General Diffusion of Knowledge"

      m. Rockfish Gap Report

      n. decentralized local authority

B. Write a well-ordered essay, 2-3 pages in length, in response to an assigned number of the following questions. Your essay, like the responses required of the questions at the end of each chapter of your text, requires you to take a position on a socio-educational issue and then defend that position with reasoned argument and evidence from the text and from other sources at your disposal. In each essay, you are expected to:

      a. clearly state your position or thesis;

      b. respond to *all parts* of the assigned question;

      c. defend your position with evidence and reasoned argument;

      d. demonstrate college-level writing skills.

1. Explain how Thomas Jefferson's educational proposals were related to both the political economy of post-Revolutionary Virginia and to Classical Liberalism.

2. Discuss the meritocratic aspects of Jefferson's educational proposals. In your essay carefully analyze which groups were disadvantaged.

3. Explain how Jefferson's educational proposals reflect a number of internal tensions in classical liberalism and how these tensions were affected by contemporary economic conditions.

4. "With all of its defects Jefferson's educational proposals represented real potential progress for post-Revolutionary Virginia." Discuss this quote.

5. The idea of educating the "citizen" was central to all of Jefferson's educational ideals. Discuss Jefferson's concept of the "citizen" and show how it was reflected in his educational proposals.

6. Explain Classical Liberalism's ideal of intellectual freedom. What paradox did this ideal present of Jefferson and other revolutionary leaders in their view of the role school s should play in the new nation? Explain.

MULTIPLE-CHOICE ITEMS

For each item, select the *best* answer from the four alternatives presented, as supported by your textbook. Students are encouraged to defend answers other than those in the answer key with evidence and argument, which may or may not prove compelling enough to have an alternate answer counted as correct.

1. During the early republic, the western frontier represented important hopes and expectations, as best described by which of the following?
   a. opportunities for wealth
   b. upward mobility
   c. self-sufficiency
   d. all of the above

2. During the early nineteenth century, which of these best describes the most influential institution for the transmission of values?
   a. family
   b. peers
   c. schooling
   d. all of the above

3.   "Patriarchy" refers to social traditions in which
   a.   women's legal status is not equal to that of men
   b.   women's perceived "worth" is not equal to that of men
   c.   men hold greater decision-making power than women
   d.   all of the above

4.   Revolutionary era Americans valued self-sufficiency and at the same time
     accepted, or at least expected, some community or court interference in
     family matters. The combination of these two concepts can be
   a.   consistent with classical liberalism
   b   consistent with an agrarian society
   c.   consistent with patriarchy
   d.   all of the above

5.   As part of the dominant ideology of the early Republic, the concept
     "representative government" was
   a.   similarly defined and described by everyone
   b.   variously defined and debated
   c.   identical to that developed in Great Britain
   d.   all of the above

6.   A hierarchical society was sharply manifested in
   a.   colonial America
   b.   feudal times
   c.   post-revolutionary America
   d.   all of the above

7.   Which of these is (are) the least significant dimension(s) of the social
     context of the post-Revolutionary era?
   a.   political economy
   b.   schools
   c.   ideology
   d.   all of the above

8. Commerce contributed to the breakdown of feudalism because
   a. it provided a mechanism for many lower class people to become upper class
   b. it eliminated social and economic hierarchy
   c. it broadened opportunities for the introduction of new ideas
   d. all of the above

9. Which of these would be *least* likely to have an educational system that offered different educational experiences to children from different economic classes?
   a. Jefferson's Virginia plan
   b. a participatory democracy in which differences in race, gender and economic status were minimized
   c. Contemporary America
   d. all of the above

10. The rise of science as a guide to action seemed logical to the liberals of the young republic because
    a. science was perceived to yield facts and truths while religion did not
    b. most citizens attended schools and were taught science there
    c. the capacity for scientific thought seemed to be a God-given ability that allowed humans to understand the God-created regularity of the natural world around them
    d. all of the above

11. Classical liberals focused on improvement here on earth because
    a. religion was not important in their lives
    b. the Puritan background emphasized doing good to each other
    c. they had a faith in human reason
    d. all of the above

12. Classical liberals' conception of sin and vice included the notion that
    a. vice should be punished by hard work
    b. religion would lead people away from sin
    c. sin and vice were an outgrowth of ignorance
    d. all of the above

13. Early classical liberals believed that revolution might be necessary because
    a. social institutions might develop which work against the general welfare
    b. the poor and unrepresented need a vehicle for social mobility
    c. revolution was seen as necessary for progress
    d. all of the above

14. Which of these is closely related to negative freedom?
    a. laissez-faire economic policy
    b. separation of church and state
    c. civil rights
    d. all of the above

15. Which of these is not consistent with Jefferson's advocacy of education?
    a. a free marketplace of ideas
    b. separation of church and state
    c. a state-approved textbook list for all districts
    d. all of the above

16. Education was valued by Jefferson in part because he believed
    a. the truth could be discovered by inquiry
    b. it would foster healthy differences of opinion
    c. it contributed to happiness
    d. all of the above

17. Jefferson's support for agrarianism is most closely linked to
    a. religious toleration
    b. individual self-sufficiency
    c. slavery
    d. all of the above

18. During his time, Jefferson's advocacy of the natural aristocracy was consistent with
    a. conservatism
    b. liberalism
    c. egalitarianism
    d. all of the above

19. Jefferson believed that education
    a. could be adequately achieved for most people in three years of schooling
    b. should be a lifelong enterprise
    c. should be provided primarily for the natural aristocracy
    d. all of the above

20. Jefferson's views on the education of women were
    a. consistent with classical liberalism
    b. inconsistent with classical liberalism
    c. irrelevant to classical liberalism
    d. all of the above

21. Jefferson's justification of his slaveholding, on the grounds that slaves were incapable of self-government, reflects
    a. the influence of classical liberalism racism
    b. Jefferson's efforts to rationalize an apparent inconsistency in his own beliefs and actions
    c. probable influence of economic considerations on Jefferson's political thought
    d. all of the above

22. Jefferson's desire to provide agrarian education to Native Americans reflects
    a. the economic priorities of the times
    b. the belief that an agrarian life instilled the best values
    c. ethnocentrism
    d. all of the above

23. Voting against Jefferson's educational proposal, his contemporaries cited it as "unnecessarily egalitarian." This term best reflects a commitment to
    a. hierarchy
    b. feudalism
    c. dualism
    d. all of the above

24. To understand important concepts such as democracy and freedom, we must seek understanding within the context in which they are advocated. This means we
    a. need to understand history
    b. need to understand ideology
    c. need to understand political economy
    d. all of the above

25. Benjamin Rush advocated that every citizen has a duty to "subdue and forget his own heart." This best reflects
    a. nationalism
    b laissez-faire
    c individualism
    d. all of the above

26. Rush claimed that teaching people to "embrace, with equal affection, the whole family of mankind" was repugnant to human nature. This best reflects
    a. nationalism
    b. laissez-faire
    c. individualism
    d. all of the above

27. Rush wanted teachers to be the absolute authority in the classroom, thus preparing youth for their subordination to laws. This reflects his belief that education should, in part, focus on
    a. individual ability
    b. citizenship
    c. intellectual freedom
    d. all of the above

28. Rush sought to convert men into "republican machines. This must be done, if we expect them to perform their parts properly, in the great machine of the government of the state." Despite the severe tone of the statement, which of the following is probably **not** reflected in it?
    a. liberalism
    b. totalitarianism
    c. nationalism
    d. all of the above

Answer Key

1. D	2. A	3. D	4. D	5. B
6. D	7. B	8. C	9. B	10. C
11. C	12. C	13. A	14. D	15. C
16. D	17. B	18. B	19. B	20. A
21. D	22. D	23. A	24. D	25. A
26. A	27. B	28. B		

Chapter 3

School as Public Institution: The Common School Era

CHAPTER OBJECTIVES

Among the objectives that Chapter 3 seeks to achieve are these:

1. Students should understand the contrasts between the political economy of Jefferson's agrarian Virginia and the urban centers in Massachusetts, and how each created different conditions for the growth of common schools.

2. Students should understand how a wide range of components interacted in the political economy of Massachusetts during the common school era, and that it was not the case that Irish Immigration alone, nor the beginnings of industry alone, nor the Jacksonian Revolution alone, but a combination of these and other factors that created fertile ground for common school legislation. Students should be engaged in *evaluating* the degree to which Mann's response to these cultural conditions was necessarily the best one (see teaching tips below).

3. Students should recognize that the political economic conditions above did not *in themselves* result in or determine necessary outcomes in school reform, but that certain people in positions of influence made sense of those political-economic conditions in particular ways, interpreted them as problematic according to their own particular values, and arrived at particular solutions as a result of these interpretations. In evaluating the ideological orientations of Mann and his Protestant allies, students should seek to understand the ideological framework of religion, republicanism, and capitalism within which the school reformers operated.

4. Students should become acquainted as much as possible with the mind and career of Horace Mann not in order to venerate him, but to understand the dominant ideology of his historical setting. They should be engaged in evaluating the degree to which

Mann's ideological orientation, particularly toward democracy, was or was not consistent with Jefferson's democratic ideals.

5. Students should understand and *evaluate* how Mann and others thought the specific curriculum of the common schools would address the cultural needs of Massachusetts at that time.

6. Students should assess the degree to which Mann's conception of the teacher, and of teacher education, was adequate for that time and for our own.

7. Students should assess the degree to which consideration of such variables as gender, race, ethnicity, religion, and economic class raise questions about the common schools and the normal schools that might not otherwise be considered.

CHAPTER OVERVIEW

An understanding of the beginning of common schooling in the United States requires attention to such social changes as urbanization, early industrialization, and patterns of immigration, all in the northeastern United States. Ideologically, the common school era was rooted in classical liberalism, which had practical consequences in urban New England different from those in rural Jeffersonian Virginia, due to differences in the political economy as well as shifts in religious thought. While Jefferson had encountered difficulty gaining consensus for a state-funded but locally-controlled school system, Horace Mann sought a state-funded and state-*controlled* school system. Due in part to the contrasts in political economy between Massachusetts and Virginia, and in part to differences between the paternalistic Whig liberalism of urban Massachusetts and the more laissez-faire liberalism of agrarian Virginia, Mann succeeded.

The interaction of political economy and ideology is sharply illustrated in U.S. citizen responses to Irish immigration. The moral and cultural judgments made by New Englanders about the Irish Catholics, and the way schooling was used as a solution to the "Irish problem," illustrates one way of responding to cultural diversity. The efforts of Mann and others to use the schools to shape the character of Massachusetts youth for moral uprightness as well as greater social stability are detailed in this chapter. Mann's efforts to create a genuine system of education through common schools as well as normal schools leads to a discussion of Mann's conception of the occupation of teaching and how teachers should be educated.

TEACHING SUGGESTIONS

1. Although the students cannot yet see it at this point in the volume, there are some ways in which Mann can be seen as a transitional figure from Jeffersonian democratic localism to modern liberal paternalism. This chapter has no specific section headed "Ideology," and students might miss the significance of Mann's ideological orientation if they are not specifically asked to think about it. They should be engaged in seeing how Mann's commitments to the primary tenets of Classical Liberalism identified in Chapter 2--natural law, rationality, virtue, progress, nationalism, education, and freedom--identify him as a classical liberal yet separate him from Jefferson in specific ways. Students should thus be reminded that Classical Liberalism was not a specific doctrine and that differences existed between Jefferson and some of his classical liberal protagonists in his own era.

2. The religious issue is an interesting one that gives insight into the culture of urban Massachusetts in terms of both ideology and political economy. Students should be asked to evaluate Mann's position on public tax support for schools that were non-sectarian Protestant in orientation but not for schools that were Catholic. Note especially the critical leverage provided by the Orestes Brownson selection. Students can think and talk about the legacy of that policy today, as well; why shouldn't tax dollars be used to support any or all schools that have religious orientations?

3. The Brownson reading illustrates a view of democracy that clearly competes with Mann's, and Brownson is familiar with the Prussian influence on Mann's thought. Students should be asked to evaluate Brownson's critique of Mann, because it calls into questions Mann's views on democracy and education, and students need to begin thinking about where they themselves stand on these concepts.

ESSAY QUESTIONS

Below are two kinds of essay questions:

a.   short essays or identification questions in which students are asked to write a descriptive paragraph or two to demonstrate their understanding of certain concepts, events, or practices; and

b   longer essays, which allow students to demonstrate their ability to analyze more complex issues involving several events, concepts, and/or practices.

A. Identify and briefly indicate the significance of an assigned number of the following:

a. Orestes Brownson
b. normal schools
c. human capital
d. feminization of teaching
e. teacher as exemplar
f. volkschule
g. Johann Fichte
h. Irish immigration
i. urbanization
j. industrial morality
k. Jacksonian Revolution
l. Westward Migration

B. Write a well-ordered essay, 2-3 pages in length, in response to an assigned number of the following questions. Your essay, like the responses required of the questions at the end of each chapter of your text, requires you to take a position on a socio-educational issue and then defend that position with reasoned argument and evidence from the text and from other sources at your disposal. In each essay, you are expected to:

a. clearly state your position or thesis;
b. respond to *all parts* of the assigned question;
c. defend your position with evidence and reasoned argument;
d. demonstrate college-level writing skills.

1. Describe what Horace Mann meant when he called the common school the "great balance wheel of society". In your essay explain how demographic and economic developments affected Mann's ideas.

2. Explain how the political economy of Massachusetts favored the development of the common school.

3. The development of normal schools was central to Horace Mann's educational proposals. Show why this was the case. In your essay demonstrate the relative importance of Mann's concern for social harmony, economic developments and theological changes in his concern for teacher training.

4. Analyze the "Irish Problem" in terms of 19th century American ideology and political economy and discuss the merits and/or weaknesses of Horace Mann's call for the common schools to solve this "problem".

5. Discuss Horace Mann's ideas for a new "pedagogy of love". In your essay explain why Mann wanted to change school discipline and the effect these changes would have on teachers and students. Analyze the appropriateness of this "pedagogy of love" for schools in a democratic society.

6. The idea of educating the "citizen" was central to Horace Mann's educational ideals. Discuss Mann's concept of the "citizen" and show how it was reflected in his educational proposals.

MULTIPLE-CHOICE ITEMS

For each item, select the *best* answer from the four alternatives presented, as supported by your textbook. Students are encouraged to defend answers other than those in the answer key with evidence and argument, which may or may not prove compelling enough to have an alternate answer counted as correct.

1. Many attempts at social reform during the common school era were guided by humanitarian concerns. This humanitarian emphasis was largely a result of

   a. popular skepticism about people being able to take control of their own destiny

   b. a sense of religious obligation

   c. increase in scientific discoveries

   d. all of the above.

2. With the development and expansion of industrialization came

   a. a larger gap between the rich and the poor

   b. a need for a cultural shift in the work ethic

   c. increased employment opportunities for women

   d. all of the above

3. Increased consumer demand during the common school era was fueled by

   a. immigration

   b. expanded transportation

   c. westward migration

   d. all of the above

4. Craftspeople moved to the urban centers because

   a. they preferred to be closer to their markets

   b. they saw the opportunity to expand their markets

   c. they relied on merchants to develop their markets

   d. all of the above

5. Industrialists provided important support for public schooling because

   a. they thought it would provide them with a larger pool of available workers

   b. they thought it would help people accept the prevailing organization of society

   c. they thought it would help to enculturate the pool of immigrant workers

   d. all of the above

6.   One of the reasons for conflict over reform efforts during the common school era was
   a. a contradiction between the idea of broadening the authority of the state on behalf of social welfare programming and the idea of individualism
   b. conflict between religious authority and state authority
   c. a concern for social harmony
   d. all of the above

7.   Focusing efforts on achieving social harmony most likely could lead to
   a. encouraging individualism
   b. encouraging conformity
   c. encouraging religious toleration
   d. all of the above

8.   Which of these would Horace Mann likely not have focused his efforts on?
   a. social cohesion
   b. further extending the franchise
   c. teacher authority
   d. all of the above

9.   Resistance to Mann's "common elements" approach came from
   a. those wanting a strict division between church and state
   b. those wanting their own religion to be taught in schools
   c. those fearing that no religion would be taught in schools
   d. all of the above

10. John Stuart Mill's statement that "Education provided by the public must be education for all..." was made in regard to his concern that
   a. public schooling should be made available to all people
   b. public schooling should provide all people with the same kind of education
   c. public schooling should be secular
   d. all of the above

11. The rise of Catholic schools can be seen as a response to
    a. Catholics' belief that academic standards would be lower in public schools
    b. anti-Catholic sentiments of the majority of common school supporters
    c. common school supporters' insistence on separation between church and state
    d. all of the above

12. Johann Fichte's position that "You must fashion [the child]...in such a way that he cannot will otherwise than you wish him to will" is most importantly tied to Mann's support for
    a. a pedagogy of love
    b. common elements
    c. teacher authority
    d. all of the above

13. Mann's belief that women would make better teachers than men reflects
    a. his concern to keep educational costs low, since women were paid less than men
    b. his belief that men as teachers were not good role models for youths
    c. his belief that women and men have inherently different natures
    d. all of the above

14. The curriculum which Mann proposed for the normal schools reflected his concern to
    a. have improved academic preparation of teachers
    b. have teachers who could learn and apply appropriate techniques of teaching
    c. credentialize the teaching profession
    d. all of the above

15. Economic justifications for schooling include the idea(s) that
    a. education is a vehicle for social mobility
    b. everyone will be trained for high-level occupations
    c. education will equalize incomes
    d. all of the above

16. Supporters of the common school movement emphasized schooling's ability to
    a. improve the morality of the population
    b. teach needed workplace skills
    c. balance inequalities of wealth
    d. all of the above

17. An economic justification of schooling often includes the view that
    a. acquisition of wealth goes to those who merit it
    b. more schooling increases the chances that innovations will occur
    c. schooling increases economic productivity
    d. all of the above

18. A shift from a barter economy to a market economy
    a. began well before the Common school movement in Massachusetts
    b. began during the Common School movement in Massachusetts
    c. was a direct result of the Massachusetts Common School movement
    d. all of the above

19. Brownson's opposition to Mann's normal school concept stemmed from his
    a. state's rights position
    b. advocacy of democratic localism
    c. belief that a variety of religious beliefs should be included in the curriculum
    d. all of the above

20. An emphasis on human capital theory
    a. accepts social class stratification
    b. argues against social class stratification
    c. proposes that schooling can eliminate inequality
    d. all of the above

21. Common schooling was seen as one solution to the "immigrant problem" because of perceptions that
    a. immigrants were uneducated and needed to learn skills necessary for democratic participation
    b. immigrants' value systems did not include the work ethic required for industrialization
    c. immigrants did not usually provide an education for their children
    d. all of the above

22. Women's opportunities for employment as teachers increased during the Common School era primarily because
    a. more teachers were needed and women represented an untapped human resource
    b. common school supporters recognized that women were the primary teachers in the home
    c. the primary characteristic of women was perceived as nurturers
    d. all of the above

23. Common schooling was widely perceived as an effort to
    a. decrease social discord
    b. increase social inequality
    c. increase political participation
    d. all of the above

24. Jefferson and Mann would probably agree on
    a. taxpayer funding of education
    b states sovereignty in matters of education
    c. different kinds of education, according to merit
    d. all of the above

25. Jefferson differed from Mann in his concern(s) about
    a. social stability
    b informed decision making
    c. the tyranny of the majority
    d. all of the above

26. For Brownson, "special" education referred to
    a. the need to fit education to the needs of the child
    b. vocational education
    c. life-long education
    d. all of the above

27. Brownson's position that every child had a "natural right to the best education..." reflects his belief that
    a. every state should regulate education
    b. all human beings have the capacity for developing their intellectual capacities
    c. education should be determined by the needs of the child
    d. all of the above

28. Brownson represents a focus on education as
    a. the right of all people
    b. the means to social mobility
    c. inculcating common values
    d. all of the above

29. Brownson's opposition to normal schools was that
    a. they would not encourage social reform
    b. they would increase the power of the already-powerful segments of society
    c. they would not contribute to social equality
    d. all of the above

30. Mann's "common elements" emphasis contributed most evidently to
    a. centralization of authority
    b. social cohesion
    c. cultural pluralism
    d. all of the above

31. In today's schooling climate Brownson would be most likely to support
    a. busing to achieve racial balance in schools
    b. enhancement programs for gifted and talented children
    c. parent councils in schools
    d. all of the above

Answer Key

1. B	2. D	3. D	4. D	5. D
6. D	7. B	8. B	9. D	10. A
11. B	12. A	13. D	14. D	15. A
16. D	17. D	18. A	19. B	20. A
21. D	22. D	23. A	24. D	25. A
26. B	27. B	28. A	29. A	30. A
31. C				

Chapter 4

Schooling and Social Inequality: The Booker T. Washington Solution

CHAPTER OBJECTIVES

Among the objectives that Chapter 4 seeks to achieve are these:

1. This chapter should equip students to understand selected dimensions of African-American history immediately following the Civil War. In particular, students should consider the nature of the racist oppression that was supported by legal measures taken in that period.

2. Students can begin to assess the degree to which political and economic power can be wielded purposefully to the advantage of some groups at the extreme expense of others, and that progress, contrary to classical liberal views, is not always inevitable.

3. Students should begin to assess the degree to which African-Americans themselves effectively took responsibility for their own education following the Civil War, and the degree to which the efforts of whites interfered with black educational achievements.

4. Students should be equipped to evaluate the degree to which, in the context of racist political economy and ideology, Booker T. Washington's educational solutions adequately served the interests of African-Americans.

5. Students should also assess the degree to which Washington's faith in social reform through educational means was adequate.

6. Students should be equipped to evaluate the critique of Washington and others formulated by W. E. B. DuBois, and to intelligently discuss whether DuBois's assessment of the problems of African-Americans was more or less adequate than Washington's assessment.

CHAPTER OVERVIEW

Chapter 4 examines the relationships between political economy, ideology, and schooling in the experience of African-Americans following the Civil War. Selected political economic developments of the period included: the Thirteenth, Fourteenth, and Fifteenth Amendments to the Constitution, which granted civil and political rights to ex-slaves and other African-Americans; the period of Reconstruction, in which African-Americans achieved significant political power in the South and during which a number of higher education institutions were established for African-Americans; and the subsequent period of "Redemption," in which the oppression of African-Americans by southern whites through "Jim Crow" laws and state constitutional revisions reached tragic proportions. Ideologically, racist European-Americans believed they were justified in their oppression of African-Americans on the basis of a "scientific" view that European-Americans were biologically more evolved than African-Americans and that classical liberal commitments to freedom and equality did not therefore apply to these "less evolved" human beings.

In terms of schooling, it is noteworthy that African-Americans themselves were remarkably successful during the Reconstruction period in establishing schools for Black children throughout the South. In general, southern Whites had less access to quality education than southern Blacks. The Redemption period, however, and particularly the period marked by the ascendancy of Booker T. Washington to political and educational power, resulted in significantly reduced opportunities for the education of African-American youth. While he is often regarded as a hero of African-American advancement, this chapter shows that Booker T. Washington's commitment to vocational education and acceptance of disfranchisement and lack of civil rights for African-Americans was opposed by some Black leaders, including W. E. B. DuBois. The contrasts between the social, political, and educational analyses of Booker T. Washington and W. E. B. DuBois are drawn in some detail and underscored in the Primary Source Reading by DuBois.

TEACHING SUGGESTIONS

1. It is our experience that this material elicits strongly-felt responses from students, some in favor of Booker T. Washington's gradualism and some in favor of W. E. B. DuBois's more confrontational politics. It is helpful to have students consider whether their own liberal faith in progress is a justifiable defense of Washington's approach. Discussions of the degree to which Jim Crow South thrived until the confrontational

politics of the Civil Rights era in the 1950s and 1960s can be useful. Nonetheless, it is difficult for students, even when they find themselves sympathetic to DuBois's radicalism, to formulate strong criticisms of Washington, whose ideology tends to mirror so closely liberal ideology of today.

2. In the Concluding Remarks section, there are five italicized questions about the relationships between education and social conditions. Part of the reason for this is to help students begin to question just how much can be accomplished toward social reform in schools themselves. One emerging theme that runs throughout much of this textbook is the tendency of liberal ideology to try to achieve significant social reform through schooling, a tendency which may well assign tasks to teachers that they are ill-positioned to achieve. This theme comes through strongly in the Progressive Era, in the post-Sputnik reform era, and in our current school reform era, and it is fruitful to raise it in the context of the Washington-DuBois debate.

3. Although the detailed exhibits in the middle of the chapter can be daunting, they should be used to focus students on the evidence that "disadvantaged" populations may well be able to meet their own educational needs, if given the opportunity, and that "advantaged" populations, acting in a liberal, paternalist model, may further erode the position of the "disadvantaged."

ESSAY QUESTIONS

Below are two kinds of essay questions:

a. short essays or identification questions in which students are asked to write a descriptive paragraph or two to demonstrate their understanding of certain concepts, events, or practices; and

b. longer essays, which allow students to demonstrate their ability to analyze more complex issues involving several events, concepts, and/or practices.

A. Identify and briefly indicate the significance of an assigned number of the following:
   a. Black Codes
   b. the Fourteenth Amendment
   c. Reconstruction
   d. Ku Klux Klan

     e. Jim Crow laws

     f. Atlanta Exposition address

     g. Tuskegee Machine

     h. Samuel Chapman Armstrong

     i. Booker T. Washington

     j. W.E.B. DuBois

B. Write a well-ordered essay, 2-3 pages in length, in response to an assigned number of the following questions. Your essay, like the responses required of the questions at the end of each chapter of your text, requires you to take a position on a socio-educational issue and then defend that position with reasoned argument and evidence from the text and from other sources at your disposal. In each essay, you are expected to:

     a. clearly state your position or thesis;

     b. respond to *all parts* of the assigned question;

     c. defend your position with evidence and reasoned argument;

     d. demonstrate college-level writing skills.

1. Critically analyze W.E.B. DuBois's criticism of Booker T. Washington's social and educational proposals for African Americans.

2. Discuss the development of education in the South during the Reconstruction era and the decade following its end.

3. Describe and evaluate the educational ideals and practices at Tuskegee and Hampton.

4. Imagine yourself a student about to graduate from Tuskegee Institute in 1900. Write a letter to a friend urging him/her to come either to Tuskegee or to the liberal-arts oriented Fisk University.

5. Critically analyze Dudley Randall's poem "Booker T. and W.E.B." (page 104 in your text).

MULTIPLE-CHOICE ITEMS

For each item, select the *best* answer from the four alternatives presented, as supported by your textbook. Students are encouraged to defend answers other than those in the answer key with evidence and argument, which may or may not prove compelling enough to have an alternate answer counted as correct.

1. During the Reconstruction period, blacks, especially southern blacks, saw many changes in their lives, except for which of the following?
   a. a constitutional amendment giving them the franchise
   b. genuine social equality with whites
   c. increased access to formal education
   d. all of the above

2. During the "period of redemption" there was a significant lowering of the status previously achieved by blacks in the Reconstruction period. This was primarily accomplished through
   a. state and federal legal decisions
   b. extra-legal mechanisms
   c. withdrawal of federal troops from the south
   d. all of the above

3. The combination of literacy and poll-tax requirements was a deadly blow to the political participation of blacks in the south because
   a. although able to cast a ballot, perhaps with coaching from a trusted friend, many voters were not yet able to read or recite materials selected for the test of literacy
   b. although able to pass the literacy test, many voters were unable to raise the amount of money required as a "tax" to cast a ballot
   c. the tests were applied in ways that specifically disfranchised black citizens
   d. all of the above

4. If a parallel can be drawn between the attitude of common school supporters toward immigrants, and the attitude toward blacks held by southern whites during the period of redemption, it could be characterized as
    a. let us provide education to you in order to bring you into the mainstream of American life
    b. we need you to be productive in the workforce
    c. we can help you to overcome your vices
    d. all of the above

5. In the name of equality and justice, Alabama and other southern states sought to provide school funding that was
    a. apportioned to black schools and white schools according to the number of students enrolled
    b. apportioned in favor of white schools
    c. roughly equivalent for both types of schools
    d. all of the above

6. In the southern states during Reconstruction, advances in blacks' access to formal schooling came largely from
    a. church groups, missionaries, and humanitarian reformers who brought to the former slaves a desire for education
    b. efforts of the North to bring the South into compliance with the new U.S. educational policies
    c. an extension of the educational efforts blacks developed during slavery
    d. all of the above

7. The gains made in public schooling by southern blacks during Reconstruction came as a direct result of
    a. blacks' active political participation
    b. federal troops enforcement of blacks' civil rights
    c. an increase in democratic sentiments in the south
    d. all of the above

8. In the United States, one democratic principle is that of majority rule, yet this sometimes results in inequalities of protection under the law. This situation
    a. is an inherent danger in a democracy
    b. is undemocratic
    c. can be rectified through the judicial process
    d. all of the above

9. Although former slaves and other blacks were given the right to vote by the Fifteenth Amendment, in the period following Reconstruction and thereafter, many of the educational gains they had achieved were eroded or lost. This can be traced to
    a. an increase in blacks' political participation
    b. decreasing black interest in formal education
    c. a lowering of blacks' power to exert political influence
    d. all of the above

10. Losing ground during the period of redemption, southern blacks
    a. continued their efforts to provide education for their children
    b. tended to give up their desire for equality
    c. focused primarily on economic gains
    d. all of the above

11. During the period of redemption, blacks' educational efforts stemmed from
    a. a continuation of their traditional desire for education
    b. a new awareness that education was the key to economic success
    c. enlisting the cooperation of monied whites
    d. all of the above

12. Prior to the Civil War there was little or no formal schooling provided for southern blacks. This was due to
    a. social Darwinist ideology
    b. economic imperatives of the South
    c. deprivation of black people's civil rights
    d. all of the above

13. The Freedmen's campaign for universal schooling can best be described as being motivated by
    a. democratic concerns
    b. concerns influenced by racial interests
    c. social mobility concerns
    d. all of the above

14. Booker T. Washington's "Atlanta Compromise" speech calling for the advancement of public education was made as
    a. an argument aligned with human capital theory
    b. an economic justification for education of blacks
    c. a call to bring blacks into useful employment
    d. all of the above

15. A statue of Booker T. Washington is said to portray him as "lifting the veil of ignorance from the Negro race." This reflects
    a. the historical consensus on Washington's contribution
    b. social Darwinism
    c. the power of myth in history
    d. all of the above

16. Which of these can be understood as resistance to undemocratic practices?
    a. black workers withdrawing from the labor market
    b. migration of blacks to the north
    c. blacks' efforts on behalf of universal education
    d. all of the above

17. The practice of noncooperation with southern white authorities by blacks
    a. accorded with Jefferson's political views
    b. was technically undemocratic
    c. was unsuccessful in extending their educational opportunities
    d. all of the above

18. During Booker T. Washington's time, a prevailing explanation for the unequal distribution of wealth and power
    a. did not take into account the effects of institutionalized racism
    b. was supported by a social Darwinist theory of evolution
    c. was based on white experience in organizing society
    d. all of the above

19. In Booker T. Washington's time it was true that American whites had long experience in organizing the forces around them, and that American blacks had long suffered degradation. These facts reflect
    a. the lack of social organization inherent in American slave culture
    b. the effects of institutional racism
    c. an unanticipated result of laissez-faire
    d. all of the above

20. Booker T. Washington's statement that "The Indian refused to submit...and to learn the white man's ways. The result is that...American Indians have disappeared....The Negro, wiser and more enduring than the Indian, patiently endured slavery [and therefore has] a civilization vastly superior to that of the Indian" reflects Washington's belief(s) that
    a. the people of both of these groups survived only to the extent that they fulfilled the economic needs of the society
    b. slavery had been mostly beneficial for the slaves
    c. blacks were inherently superior to American Indians
    d. all of the above

21. Booker T. Washington's counsel to blacks can be characterized most accurately as
    a. cooperation with whites
    b. resistance to whites
    c. complete acquiescence to whites
    d. all of the above

22. Booker T. Washington's belief in the connection between property and morality is similar to the beliefs of
    a. Jefferson and classical liberals
    b. Mann and whig school reformers
    c. contemporary liberalism
    d. all of the above

23. Booker T. Washington's economic justification of schooling demonstrated his belief that
    a. the kind of education he advocated could effect social and political changes
    b. a market economy would not tolerate the inefficiencies of racial discrimination
    c. education would provide the key to citizenship for blacks
    d. all of the above

24. Viewing citizenship as something earned by achieving a certain level of education
    a. runs counter to American constitutional guarantees
    b. accords with American democratic principles
    c. would benefit all citizens equally
    d. all of the above

25. Booker T. Washington believed that respect and citizenship would come to blacks in proportion to their accumulation of property, education and good jobs. His own life seemed to prove this. His belief overlooks
    a. the contribution his accommodationist policies had towards his success
    b. the unrepresentativeness of his experiences
    c. the existence of institutionalized racism in his own time
    d. all of the above

26. DuBois advocated
    a. assimilation
    b. protest
    c. self-assertion
    d. all of the above

27. "Education to meet the needs of group differences" has traditionally been done under the stated or implied claim(s) of
    a. advantages for each individual child's development
    b. unfairness of having the same expectations for all children
    c. certain groups can benefit from education more than other groups can
    d. all of the above

28. "Education for what people have in common" might be
    a. democratic in practice
    b. antidemocratic in practice
    c. guided by the goal of cultural assimilation
    d. all of the above

29. DuBois criticized Washington's goals for education on the grounds that
    a. effective economic progress is unlikely if civil and political rights are restricted
    b. economic progress is not an appropriate goal for education
    c. it would not increase blacks' access to formal schooling
    d. all of the above

30. DuBois' calls for opposition to racism
    a. were similar to Jefferson's calls for opposition to an unjust government
    b. were similar to Washington's suggestions for overcoming racism
    c. counseled civil disobedience
    d. all of the above

Answer Key

1. B	2. D	3. D	4. D	5. B
6. C	7. A	8. D	9. C	10. A
11. A	12. D	13. D	14. D	15. C
16. A	17. A	18. D	19. B	20. C
21. A	22. D	23. D	24. A	25. D
26. D	27. D	28. D	29. A	30. A

Chapter 5

Education for the Vocations: The Progressive Era

CHAPTER OBJECTIVES

1. This chapter seeks to impress upon students the massive nature of the shifts in political economy, ideology, and schooling that took place at the dawn of the twentieth century and to equip students to evaluate these shifts.

2. This chapter seeks to develop in students a deeper and broader base from which they can evaluate the nature of racial and ethnic prejudice as an historical phenomenon in the Unites States. One objective here is to allow students to compare progressive educational responses to ethnic differences with the responses to African-Americans identified in Chapter 4 and the responses to Irish-Americans identified in Chapter 3.

3. Students should be equipped to assess the degree to which scientific management in the industrial workplace was in the interest of workers and was consistent with democratic ideals.

4. Students should evaluate the degree to which modern liberal ideology was consistent with specifically-articulated conceptions of democracy, such as Jeffersonian participatory democracy or Dewey's developmental democracy.

5. Students should see the degree to which domestic social order was achieved by the exercise of the force of arms and by political and economic control of schooling, thus calling into question a "consensus" theory of social order.

6. Students should be able to distinguish among different strands of progressivism and be able to evaluate the interests served by these different camps.

7. Finally, students should be able to evaluate the degree to which all population groups of students were equally well served by the four progressive educational aims of social stability, employable skills, equal educational opportunity, and meritocracy.

CHAPTER OVERVIEW

In a number of ways, Chapter 5 is a pivotal chapter for this textbook. It examines the most dramatic changes in political economy, ideology, and schooling to take place in U. S. history. If the Jeffersonian chapter treated the first fifty years of the American republic and the common schooling chapter treated the beginnings of industry and accompanying transitions in classical liberalism of the next fifty years, then Chapter 5, in its focus on the half-century from the 1870s to the 1920s, unveils the modern era in American culture and schooling. Chief political-economic changes included: the emergence of a largely urban society, immigration from new sources in Asian and southern and eastern Europe, and far-reaching new developments in industrialization and monopoly capitalism. Ideologically, classical liberalism became transformed by political, economic, and intellectual developments into a new form of liberalism, variously termed "new," "modern," or "corporate" liberalism. This revised liberalism maintained commitments to scientific rationality, progress, and freedom, but it transformed these commitments to be consistent with the need of the emerging leaders of government and business to justify expert and bureaucratic control and social, political, and economic institutions in American culture.

The chapter's first page uses the Gary school system as an illustration of how schools themselves were transformed, and how this transformation was publically justified during the Progressive period. School reform became a major priority on the national agenda for members of the business community, journalists, social reformers, educators, and educational psychologists who began to explain human learning in decidedly new terms. As a result of these reform efforts, new objectives for schooling emerged, including: training students with employable skills in the industrial workforce; enhancing social stability through an education that would adjust students to the political and economic hierarchies of the twentieth century; providing a form of equal educational opportunity that assumed markedly different talents among students and offered different curricula for those different talents; and, finally, establishing a system of meritocracy that would appear to make different educational outcomes contingent only upon the talent and effort of the students themselves. To achieve these objectives, schools changed sharply in the Progressive Era in terms of who was required to attend school, the different curricula

① changes in   ② change in

offered to the students who attended, the establishment of extra-curricular activities for social and educational aims, and the shift in control of schools from local neighborhoods to centralized school boards dominated by business and professional class membership and ideology.

TEACHING SUGGESTIONS

1. A key to students' understanding of the nature of modern liberalism is for them to get clear on the distinctive use of that term in this volume. In this account, "modern liberalism" includes liberals and conservatives, republicans and democrats (the narrow ideological range of ideas viable in dominant American political and economic institutions is discussed at length in Chapter 8). Just as there was a wide range of political positions present among members of the Constitutional Convention in the 19th Century, all of whom were classical liberals, so is there a range of political positions identifiable under the broad descriptor "modern liberal" today. "Conservatives" today like to ground their arguments on a more Jeffersonian foundation than their "liberal" counterparts, but all of them tend to subscribe to the components of modern liberal ideology, with its commitments (for example) to decision-making by experts, business/government collaboration, and relativist rather than absolute approach to the nature of truth. All of these have replaced the tenets of classical liberalism as "taken for granteds" among institutional leaders in the U.S. Students should understand that the label "modern liberal" thus refers to broad ideological conceptions of the nature of truth, reality, virtue, and freedom rather than to political differences within those conceptions.

2. In particular, the five questions raised in the concluding discussion of Chapter 4 are fruitful guides to discussion in Chapter 5. Again, they tend to focus on the degree to which education can effectively address deep-rooted social, political, and economic problems.

3. It is our experience that students have very little experience using the concept "democracy" as a well-articulated evaluative criterion. They tend to have been taught that democracy is synonymous with American society or with the American political system and are ill-equipped with a concept of democracy precise enough to allow them effectively to critique dimensions of that society or that political system with respect to how adequately democratic they are. For democracy to serve as an ethical or political

standard, students must be able to articulate some precise definitions of democracy and then choose among these definitions a yardstick by which social, educational, political, or economic policy may be measured. There are several such definitions available in the text so far. They may be derived from Jefferson's notion of citizen participation, Dewey's notion of "all-around growth of every member of society," or DuBois's comments about the soul of democracy, among others. The point here is that students have been taught to think that schools are agents of democracy in our society without understanding the concept of democracy itself, except in sloganeering terms, and this chapter offers the occasion for them to begin thinking more precisely about what democratic schooling might mean in curriculum and in governance. Who should decide what the schools should be, in a democratic society, and how should it be decided? And what forms of school experience are most consistent with democratic ideals? These questions cannot be pursued profitably unless students feel secure with some definite notion of democratic ideals themselves.

ESSAY QUESTIONS

Below are two kinds of essay questions:

   a. short essays or identification questions in which students are asked to write a descriptive paragraph or two to demonstrate their understanding of certain concepts, events, or practices; and

   b. longer essays which allow students to demonstrate their ability to analyze more complex issues involving several events, concepts, and/or practices.

A. Identify and briefly indicate the significance of an assigned number of the following:
   a. the New Immigration
   b. Origin of the Species
   c. Taylorization
   d. Populism
   e. the "new psychology"
   f. social efficiency
   g   John Dewey
   h. Charles W. Eliot
   i. Equal Educational Opportunity
   j. vocational education

B. Write a well-ordered essay, 2-3 pages in length, in response to an assigned number of the following questions. Your essay, like the responses required of the questions at the end of each chapter of your text, requires you to take a position on a socio-educational issue and then defend that position with reasoned argument and evidence from the text and from other sources at your disposal. In each essay, you are expected to:

    a. clearly state your position or thesis;

    b. respond to *all parts* of the assigned question;

    c. defend your position with evidence and reasoned argument;

    d. demonstrate college-level writing skills.

1   Critically analyze the differences between John Dewey's idea of education through the vocations and Charles W. Eliot's idea of education for the vocations.

2. What impact did the massive demographic, economic and ideological changes occurring at the turn of the twentieth century have on the development of Progressive education?

3. Explain how and why reformers centralized power in both city and school government during the progressive era. What effect, in your view, did this have on American democracy?

4. Analyze how the ideological shift from Classical Liberalism to Modern Liberalism contributed to the development of the objectives of modern schooling.

5. Why would liberal education be incompatible with the workplace requirements after Taylorization?

MULTIPLE-CHOICE ITEMS

For each item, select the *best* answer from the four alternatives presented, as supported by your textbook. Students are encouraged to defend answers other than those in the answer key with evidence and argument, which may or may not prove compelling enough to have an alternate answer counted as correct.

1. During the Progressive era, enormous changes were occurring--changes that seemed to threaten the widely held belief that America was a land of opportunity, with plenty for everyone. The new immigrants were seen as part of this challenge primarily because it was believed
   a. they took jobs away from the old immigrants
   b. they were polluting the genetic stock of America
   c. they had no valuable job skills
   d. all of the above

2. Jefferson feared that urbanization would wreak havoc on the nation. The Progressives saw an increase of crimes associated with urbanization. These two points are
   a. related in that Jefferson's and the Progressives' apprehension was that one component of urbanization would be poverty, which breeds crime
   b. unrelated in the Jefferson feared for the loss of agrarian values, and the Progressives feared for the loss of capitalistic values
   c. unrelated in that the Progressives viewed urbanization as a necessary aspect of progress
   d. all of the above

3. The rise of the factory system brought with it
   a. a need for easily replaceable workers
   b. lower pay for workers
   c. decreased self-direction for workers
   d. all of the above

4. The introduction of Taylor's scientific management in industry was aimed at
   a. increasing production
   b. diminishing workforce autonomy
   c. controlling knowledge
   d. all of the above

5. Women's opportunities for employment increased during the Progressive era primarily because

    a. their work in the home was not as important in an urban setting as it had been in an agrarian one

    b. industrialization required a larger workforce

    c. enlarged bureaucracies created clerical jobs believed to be most suitable for women

    d. all of the above

6. Worker resistance to scientific management in industry primarily was

    a. based on the fear that mechanization was endangering their livelihoods

    b. centered on issues of worker autonomy

    c. that production rose much more than their wages did

    d. all of the above

7. The handicraft system of production of goods

    a. disintegrated family and community ties

    b. discouraged self employment

    c. provided for worker autonomy

    d. all of the above

8. Opposition to the scientific management of workers came from several perspectives. Among these were advocates of

    a. agrarian localism

    b. industrial democracy

    c. trade unionism

    d. all of the above

9. Centralization of economic and political power is

    a. a feature of political-economic change in the Progressive era

    b. a clear way to achieve democratic ideals

    c. synonymous with socialism

    d. all of the above

10. The establishment of commissions that regulated the new giant corporations and monopolies
    a. resulted in regulations that protected consumers from abuse by monopolistic practices
    b. further eroded the public accountability of government agencies
    c. contributed to the decentralization of monopolistic power
    d. all of the above

11. The broadest way to characterize Progressive reforms is
    a. regulation
    b. de-centralization
    c. Taylorization
    d. all of the above

12. The results of Progressive economic reforms largely
    a. brought a market-driven economy under more government/business control
    b. protected the rest of society from abuses by the privileged few
    c. prevented the government from meddling in the affairs of business
    d. all of the above

13. Centralization of urban government was advocated in part as a way to overcome the abuses of the ward system. This change in city government had the effect(s) of
    a. further marginalizing minority groups
    b. enhancing social class stratification
    c. weakening socialism
    d. all of the above

14. Progressives' advocacy of centralization of decision making reflects their stated or implied belief(s) in
    a. social Darwinism
    b. humanitarianism
    c. depoliticization
    d. all of the above

15. Modern liberal ideology included a conception of the world around us as functioning organically. This is in sharp **contrast** to which of the following ideas?
    a. truths are unchanging
    b. decisions about social goals should be made by specialists
    c. truth can change with changes in methods for determining truth
    d. all of the above

16. Application of the scientific method for reaching reasonable conclusions
    a. was an extension of social Darwinism
    b. enhanced faith in the common person's ability to reach valid conclusions
    c. enhanced the status of experts
    d. all of the above

17. Reliance on experts to determine the best courses of social programming
    a. weakened the efficacy of the common person to be self-directed
    b. strengthened participatory democracy
    c. ensured protection of the least powerful from abuses of the ward system
    d. all of the above

18. Classical liberal emphasis on individualism was reflected in the desire for what we have termed "negative freedom." In contrast to this, the modern liberals desired
    a. government regulations to protect certain freedoms
    b. a laissez-faire government
    c. individual autonomy
    d. all of the above

19. Progressives viewed the schools as the appropriate place to solve the problems associated with industrialization, immigration and urbanization in part because
    a. schooling could produce experts
    b. non-school institutions previously depended on to instill values were mistrusted
    c. the superiority of the scientific method could be demonstrated more widely in the schools
    d. all of the above

20. The influence of the "new psychology" which rose to prominence during the Progressive era can be seen today in the method(s) of
    a. positive reinforcement (rewarding approved behaviors)
    b. school-sponsored extracurricular activities
    c. "time-out" boxes
    d. all of the above

21. The belief that people learn best while engaged in performing an activity is most like
    a. transfer-of-training assumptions
    b. vocational education assumptions
    c. liberal educational assumptions
    d. all of the above

22. Educators and others who advocated progressive education reforms held a view of the "new" students as
    a. learning through emotions more than intellect
    b. requiring guidance toward their eventual place in life
    c. learning through pursuing their own interests
    d. all of the above

23. Active citizen participation in democratic institutions is advocated by
    a. a social efficiency view of progress
    b. a developmental democracy view of progress
    c. a Progressive view of progress
    d. all of the above

24. Dewey's conception of a free individual as one who can frame and execute his or her own purposes is in sharp contrast to the concepts embedded in
    a. Progressive vocational education
    b. participatory democracy
    c. classical liberalism
    d. all of the above

25. Dewey advocated bringing into the curriculum activities based on occupations with which the students were familiar. He favored this because
    a. the industrialization of the era required that children learn trade skills as early as possible
    b. he wanted education to be more relevant to the non-school life of students
    c. he wanted education to be centered on society, not on the child
    d. all of the above

26. Eliot and others saw schooling as a way to teach students to respect experts. This can contribute to social stability because
    a. it increases the number of proposals for planning of society-level programs
    b. it decreases the probability that ineffective social programming will be pursued
    c. it encourages people to accept their lot in life
    d. all of the above

27. It has been said that the classical curriculum aimed to train all students to be President. But America requires such a tiny proportion of the population to fill this job! We need a curriculum that helps students get jobs in the existing, and predicted, economy. This line of argument represents
    a. support for vocational education
    b. a manpower model of schooling
    c. an economic justification of schooling
    d. all of the above

28. Advocates of using the schools to increase social efficiency cited society's need for a curriculum
    a. that was designed around the perceived needs of the student
    b. that encouraged respect for experts
    c. that reflected social conditions
    d. all of the above

29. Understanding "equal educational opportunity" as providing the student with the education most appropriate for his or her potential
    a. has been historically a good way to overcome societal differences resulting from economic class, ethnicity, and gender
    b. is more fair than expecting everyone to be able to master the same basic material
    c. relies to some extent on predicting the future
    d. all of the above

Answer Key

1. D	2. A	3. D	4. D	5. D
6. B	7. C	8. D	9. A	10. B
11. A	12. A	13. D	14. D	15. A
16. C	17. A	18. A	19. D	20. D
21. B	22. D	23. B	24. A	25. B
26. C	27. D	28. D	29. C	

Chapter 6

Culture and Control: Schooling and the American Indian

CHAPTER OBJECTIVES

Among the objectives that Chapter 6 seeks to achieve are these:

1. This chapter seeks to exercise students' thinking about how modern liberalism operates in the context of a specific historical problem: the coexistence of European-Americans and indigenous Americans in twentieth-century.

2. In considering this, students should evaluate the degree to which modern liberal ideology has affected American Indians' efforts to determine their own lives and futures.

3. In particular, the conflicts between modern liberal commitments to progress and Native American commitments to cultural traditions should be highlighted as students evaluate the significance of this conflict for educational policy-making. Students should be engaged in evaluating who should be responsible for determining the education of Native Americans in the twentieth century.

4. Students should evaluate the degree to which progressive education as conceived by American government officials was an appropriate response to Native American educational needs.

5. Students should employ the careers and thinking of John Collier and Willard Beatty as lenses through which to understand and evaluate the applicability of liberal educational commitments to Native American culture.

6. Students should be engaged in assessing the degree to which cultural pluralism was a more democratic educational and cultural aim than cultural assimilation for American Indians in the first half of the twentieth century.

CHAPTER OVERVIEW

Chapter 6 examines ways in which progressive liberal ideology was brought to bear in shaping educational policy for Native Americans in the 1920s through 1940s. This brief history raises questions about modern liberal commitments to cultural pluralism in which cultural and linguistic differences within a society are valued and maintained, versus a commitment to assimilation, in which the customs, habits, and languages of subcultures are absorbed into a dominant culture. It appears that the history of American Indian education since the late nineteenth century has reflected a commitment to scientific management of Indian acculturation and assimilation by European-American administrators. Part of the reason for this has been a fundamental clash between an impulse toward "manifest destiny," tempered by corporate liberal democratic ideology, and Native American approaches to life that did not emphasize liberal concepts of property, progress, scientific rationality, and nationalism. In its effort to assimilate Native Americans into the dominant ideology and economic life of twentieth century European-America, the Federal government turned to formal schooling as its primary agency of reform.

To illustrate how well-intentioned liberals sought to acculturate American Indians through scientific management, this chapter reviews the career of John Collier, who was Commissioner of Indian Affairs from 1933 to 1945. While Collier was a progressive advocate of Indian cultural values, he did not support a genuine cultural pluralism in which Native Americans could exercise self-determination regarding their cultural and educational futures. Instead, he sought to use modern psychology and administrative techniques to bring Indians to value modified forms of assimilation themselves. Collier believed that principles of progressive education could be employed to shape Native American children's attitudes more positively toward the dominant culture. Progressive educator Willard Walcott Beatty further extended Collier's commitment to assimilation through progressive education for Native American children. The Primary Source Readings at the end of the chapter contrast an administrative-progressive view of Native American social policy with a statement by Native Americans themselves about their own desire for self-determination and cultural pluralism.

TEACHING SUGGESTIONS

1. Due to an historic veneration of a "melting pot" approach to coexistence of differing cultures in the United States, it is difficult for students to conceptualize concrete implications of a commitment to cultural pluralism. This chapter offers an opportunity to discuss what pluralist social policy and pluralist educational policy might look like. One way to address this is to take seriously the notion of self-determination, which does not guarantee predictable outcomes, but which secures a commitment to democratic processes of arriving at those outcomes. Students can be engaged in productive discussion of the degree to which modern liberal commitments to scientific management of social problems may interfere with genuine pluralism and self-determination. Historical examples again may be found in the common schooling movement as well as in the Progressive Era and in American Indian educational history.

2. Unlike most of the other chapters, Chapter 6 contrasts two Primary Source Readings, one by a modern liberal administrator of Indian Affairs and the other by Native Americans themselves. These short excerpts offer provocative opportunities for textual interpretation of contrasting ideological commitments.

ESSAY QUESTIONS

Below are two kinds of essay questions:

   a. short essays or identification questions in which students are asked to write a descriptive paragraph or two to demonstrate their understanding of certain concepts, events, or practices; and

   b. longer essays, which allow students to demonstrate their ability to analyze more complex issues involving several events, concepts, and/or practices.

A. Identify and briefly indicate the significance of an assigned number of the following:

   a. pluralism
   b. assimilation
   c. dominant culture
   d. trust relationship
   e. Dawes Allotment Act

    f. Native American boarding schools

    g. the Merriam Report

    h. John Collier

    i. Self-Determination and Education Assistance Act

    j. Willard Walcott Beatty

B. Write a well-ordered essay, 2-3 pages in length, in response to an assigned number of the following questions. Your essay, like the responses required of the questions at the end of each chapter of your text, requires you to take a position on a socio-educational issue and then defend that position with reasoned argument and evidence from the text and from other sources at your disposal. In each essay, you are expected to:

    a. clearly state your position or thesis;

    b. respond to *all parts* of the assigned question;

    c. defend your position with evidence and reasoned argument;

    d. demonstrate college-level writing skills.

1. Explain how U.S. policy toward Native American Education may be seen as part of a larger cultural, social and economic conflict between native Americans and the dominant white culture.

2. Show how the educational policy of the Bureau of Indian Affairs during the 1930s-1940s may be considered "progressive".

3. Helen Hunt Jackson's book *A Century of Dishonor* describes the U.S. relations with Native American People during the 19th and early 20th centuries. Indicate why this characterization might also be an appropriate designation for U.S. policy regarding Native American Education during the twentieth century.

4. If the statement "What Indians Want" by the American Indian Chicago Conference had been the guiding philosophy of U.S. educational policy toward Native Americans, how might that policy have been different form what history has recorded? Explain.

MULTIPLE-CHOICE ITEMS

For each item, select the *best* answer from the four alternatives presented, as supported by your textbook. Students are encouraged to defend answers other than those in the answer key with evidence and argument, which may or may not prove compelling enough to have an alternate answer counted as correct.

1. Of the following, which might <u>best</u> be included in the concept of pluralism?
   a. all groups live as they choose
   b. some differences among groups are tolerated
   c. groups differences and interactions among groups are perceived as positive cultural resources for all groups
   d. all of the above.

2. Assimilationist efforts can have
   a. positive and negative impacts on the assimilated people
   b. unintended consequences
   c. good and bad impacts on the dominant culture
   d. all of the above.

3. Assimilation for Native Americans differs from assimilation of the Irish and other European groups in that
   a. Native Americans were expected to assimilate into the invading culture
   b. non-Native Americans had the advantage of accommodating to a culture identical to their own
   c. Irish and other European groups could easily resist assimilation by returning home
   d. all of the above.

4. The BIA's and others' educational attempts to assimilate Native Americans resulted in
   a. loss of cultural identity by Native Americans
   b. legal protection of Native American cultures
   c. legal restriction of Native American cultures
   d. all of the above.

5. The controlled democratic participatory rights which Native Americans have means
   a. someone else determines the options from which they may choose
   b. their options are limited by treaties which they did not understand
   c. they have fewer options because they are not U.S. citizens
   d. all of the above.

6. Why did Indians become less important to trade in the 18th century than they were earlier?
   a. the dominant culture had more interest in manufactured goods than in Indian-made ones
   b. the Indians had fewer material goods to trade
   c. there were fewer Indians with whom to trade
   d. all of the above.

7. The trading power that Indians had came from
   a. their control over their land
   b. their right to set treaties with the federal government regarding their resources
   c. their resistance to acculturation
   d. all of the above.

8. The U.S. Constitution prohibits individual states from engaging in treaties with Native Americans because
   a. treaty making with sovereign peoples is reserved to the Federal government
   b. Native Americans as a group are considered one nation
   c. the number of tribes is too large for each state to make effective policy
   d. all of the above.

9. The status of "protected" nation is grounded in
   a. paternalism
   b. ethnocentrism
   c. limited opportunity of the protected to defend their own interests
   d. all of the above.

10. Many parents tell their children to do something because "I'm older and I know what's best for you." This is in some respects similar to
    a. the concept of manifest destiny
    b. Indians' cultural practices honoring the authority of tradition
    c. religious fundamentalism
    d. all of the above.

11. Which of these aspects of U.S. government trusteeship of Native Americans has been and continues to be contested?
    a. rights of Native Americans to manage their own affairs
    b. rights of Native Americans to manage their own resources
    c. government provision of education for Native Americans
    d. all of the above.

12. In the reading by Collier we see several references to the importance of discovering what motivates the "being of the individual or group." This is a key emphasis in policies of
    a. modern liberalism
    b. the "new psychology"
    c. assimilation
    d. all of the above.

13. Collier emphasized that "deep and central preoccupations...can be helped to apply themselves to new and practical ends." This reflects liberal reformers' desire for
    a. schooling that was responsive to the Indian child's interests
    b. reducing or eliminating Indian resistance to assimilation
    c. creating a pluralist vision for schooling
    d. all of the above

14. In the authors' view, Collier's approach to scientific management of Indian education would
    a. force Indians into European knowledge and values against their wills
    b. allow Indian tribes to frame and execute their own educational purposes
    c. enlist Indians willingly into assimilationist education
    d. all of the above

15. The point of the author's attention to Collier's film censorship was that it illustrated
    a. Collier's paternalism
    b. Collier's respect for the power of art and culture as social tools
    c. Collier's zeal for values education
    d. all of the above

16. Willard Beatty's administrative progressive approach to Indian education included
    a. adjusting Indian attitudes toward manual labor
    b. educating Indians to resist dehumanizing factory conditions
    c. educating Indians first and foremost in Indian culture
    d. all of the above

17. Beatty's educational view most resembles the approach of which of the following?
    a. W.E.B. DuBois
    b. Booker T. Washington
    c. John Dewey
    d. all of the above

18. Collier's respect for "child study" in education is evidence of
    a. progressive educational ideals
    b. lingering classical liberal approaches to education
    c. a commitment to faculty psychology
    d. all of the above

19. Collier's attention to the "individual unconsciousness" of the Indian child is grounded in
    a. faculty psychology
    b. the Old Testament
    c. new psychology
    d. all of the above

20. Collier's regard for "scientific planning," "scientific evaluation," and "the science of society" are all characteristic of
    a. a disdain for expertise
    b. a veneration of expertise
    c. understanding of the truth of Indian knowledge and values
    d. all of the above

21. Collier's emphasis on "efficient and democratic administration" reflected the view that
    a. Indians should make their own decisions without bureaucratic intervention
    b. education could lead Indians to make decisions consistent with dominant European values
    c. Indians should be encouraged to vote in presidential elections
    d. all of the above

22. In "What Indians Want," the tribal authors' view of Federal withdrawal from responsibilities to Indian tribes is
    a. that such withdrawal would leave the tribes free and independent
    b. that such withdrawal would deprive tribes of needed material assistance
    c. that such withdrawal would deprive tribes of their sovereign status
    d. all of the above

23. In "What Indians Want," the concept of democratic governance expressed is most similar to that of
    a. John Collier
    b. Willard Beatty
    c. W.E.B. DuBois
    d. all of the above

24. For "life, liberty, and the pursuit of happiness," the tribal authors of "What Indians Want" believe the following is necessary
    a. a spirit of charity on the part of the federal government
    b. scientific study of their problems
    c. material assistance in developing resources and opportunities
    d. all of the above

25. Collier's emphasis on the need to make Indian education significantly more realistic was based on his
    a. expectations of their future roles in society and in the workforce
    b. belief in cultural pluralism
    c. belief that Indians needed to learn more about democracy in order to participate fully in the society they would enter after graduation
    d. all of the above

Answer Key

1. C	2. D	3. A	4. D	5. A
6. D	7. D	8. A	9. C	10. B
11. D	12. D	13. B	14. C	15. D
16. A	17. B	18. A	19. C	20. B
21. B	22. B	23. C	24. C	25. A

Chapter 7

National School Reform: The Cold War Era

CHAPTER OBJECTIVES

Among the objectives that Chapter 7 seeks to achieve are these:

1. The chapter should deepen and extend students' ability to think critically about the presuppositions underlying the structure and content of modern schooling, particularly at the secondary level.

2. Students should engage in thinking critically about how modern liberal commitments to such values as expert knowledge, meritocracy and nationalism influence schooling in the latter half of the twentieth century.

3. They should also engage in thinking critically about the school as an instrument of national political policy in the political-economic context of the United States after World War II.

4. Students should question the notion of a nationalist agenda for schooling within the context of democratic ideals, so that the idea of "national interest" can itself become problematic. Who, for example, legitimately determines what the "national interest" is in a democracy, and how does the student's answer to that question compare with the historical record of the Conant era of reform?

5. Students should consider this historical instance of how an expressed commitment to democracy and equality can, in modern liberal schooling policy, serve students inequitably.

6. Students should also consider an alternative approach to democratic education in contemporary society, one that is committed not to social or political outcomes but to an ideal of human development applicable to all students.

7. The chapter can thereby help students challenge their own tendency to believe that the dominant way of thinking about school and society in a particular era was the only "sensible" approach, or that it was a necessary "product of the times" and therefore a consensus view.

CHAPTER OVERVIEW

Chapter 7 documents the emergence of the modern American secondary school--the comprehensive high school--in the post World War II period of the United States. The analysis is grounded in the political-economic and ideological context of the Cold War, but the components of modern liberalism remain explicit. Thus, the fundamental objectives of school reform that emerged in the progressive era--employable skills, social stability, meritocracy and equal educational opportunity--remain central to the thinking of the Cold-War era reformers. Chief among these was Professor James B. Conant, President of Harvard University and later U.S. ambassador to Germany. Conant provides a lens through which the nationalism of the social and educational thinking of his day are examined. In contrast to Conant, the chapter presents a selection by Professor Mark Van Doren, who provides students with a different way to think about the central role of education in modern democratic society. This contrast suggests parallels with similar contrasts elsewhere articulated in the book--Dewey vs. Eliot, Washington vs. DuBois, Mann vs. Brownson, and others.

TEACHING SUGGESTIONS

1. For most college faculty, this chapter is the first one in the volume that describes an era in which the faculty member has considerable "lived experience." Yet, while decades of Cold War tensions are vivid and fresh in the minds of faculty members, much of that era is accessible to most college students only through historical accounts. The lived experience of the college professor can provide valuable points of insight for the student, and more importantly, it can legitimize students' reporting on their own lived experiences in the comprehensive high schools that the Conant era fostered. Students come from a variety of different kinds of secondary schools, however, and their own oral reports on their experiences of these schools can provide valuable points of comparison and contrast on such issues as ability grouping, guidance counseling, vocational education, advanced placement exams, and so on. The experiences of inner city students, suburban students, and rural students can be shown to bear striking

similarities and differences in the categories about which Conant was concerned, and student discussion of these can throw the Conant agenda into a more vivid and potentially more critical light.

2. The "taken for granteds": ideological foundations of the comprehensive high school. As students discuss the dimensions of their high school experiences, they can be engaged in discussion of how modern liberal commitments--for example, to meritocracy and equality of educational opportunity--were embodied in their school lives. Classroom debates over tracking, vocational education, and government by experts, for example, can provide ideological bridges from the Conant era to our own.

3. As always, students should be encouraged to try to discern the author's point of view-- for example, the critical perspective on Conant's Cold War justifications for school reform--and to evaluate whether that point of view is simply asserted or whether it is adequately supported by the author's analysis.

4. If students have practicum experiences associated with their coursework, they can be encouraged to isolate specific features of classroom structure or practice for observation and analysis, applying criteria from Conant's or Van Doren's recommendations as "yardsticks" by which the practice can be measured. How well does the practice identified live up to an ideal articulated by one of these educators?

5. Students have a difficult time making sense of the Van Doren article, at first. At least some classroom time should be devoted to finding those dimensions of the selection that carry the weight of the piece, that make it distinctively different from Conant. Particular time should be spent on interpreting problematic passages, keeping the question, "What did Van Doren appear to mean by this?" central to the discussion and open to competing interpretations. Most important, however, might be the effort to compare the schools of today with Van Doren's ideal of "education for all." Such a comparison might reveal that Van Doren was calling for an approach to education very different from that with which today's college students are most familiar.

ESSAY QUESTIONS

Below are two kinds of essay questions:

a. short essays or identification questions in which students are asked to write a descriptive paragraph or two to demonstrate their understanding of certain concepts, events, or practices; and

b. longer essays, which allow students to demonstrate their ability to analyze more complex issues involving several events, concepts, and/or practices.

A. Identify and briefly indicate the significance of each of the following:

a. containment
b. Senator Joseph McCarthy
c. John Birch Society
d. Sputnik
e. "provisional freedom"
f. Scholastic Aptitude Test
g. *The American High School Today*
h. Educational Testing Service
i. community college
j. life adjustment education
k. *Slums and Suburbs*
l. The GI Bill

B. Write a well-ordered essay, 2-3 pages in length, in response to an assigned number of the following questions. Your essay, like the responses required of the questions at the end of each chapter of your text, requires you to take a position on a socio-educational issue and then defend that position with reasoned argument and evidence from the text and from other sources at your disposal. In each essay, you are expected to:

a. clearly state your position or thesis;
b. respond to *all parts* of the assigned question;
c. defend your position with evidence and reasoned argument;
d. demonstrate college-level writing skills.

1. Compare the major educational recommendations of James B. Conant with those advocated by Mark Van Doren in "Education for All," assessing their relative significance for democratic life.

2. Explain the role that concerns for national security played in at least five of James B. Conant's educational proposals.

3. Critically analyze the degree to which Conant's educational recommendations might be characterized as elitist in nature.

4. Show the degree to which modern liberal ideology and modern psychology were important for Conant's educational reforms.

5. Explain why it might be argued that Conant's educational recommendations reinforced social class advantages and tended to cement existing class lines.

MULTIPLE-CHOICE ITEMS

For each item, select the *best* answer from the four alternatives presented, as supported by your textbook. Students are encouraged to defend answers other than those in the answer key with evidence and argument, which may or may not prove compelling enough to have an alternate answer counted as correct.

1. The post-WWII period in the United States was marked by
   a. economic growth
   b. stockmarket failure and economic depression
   c. strong alliances with the Soviet Union
   d. all of the above

2. Public fear of Soviet Communism
   a. was irrelevant to educational policy discussion in the 1950s
   b. fueled fears about the inadequacy of American schools
   c. helped reduce the national defense budget
   d. all of the above

3. In the Cold War era, centralized and expert decision-making
   a. was subject to general mistrust
   b. no longer conflicted with democratic ideals
   c. was viewed as a direct route to progress
   d. all of the above

4. President Dwight D. Eisenhower's reference to the "military-industrial complex" was intended to describe
   a. Soviet communism
   b. higher education in America
   c. the postwar political economy of the United States
   d. all of the above

5. Conant's support of the SAT was consistent with
   a. a social efficiency approach to education
   b. a belief in scientific measurement of inherent abilities
   c. new liberal ideology
   d. all of the above

6. The success of the G.I. Bill of Rights demonstrated that
   a. Conant's assumptions about talent were questionable
   b. the SAT is a reliable predictor of college success
   c. the federal government should leave educational policy to the states
   d. all of the above

7. As Harvard's president, Conant viewed vocational education as
   a. anti-intellectual
   b. anti-democratic
   c. consistent with equality of opportunity
   d. all of the above

8. The Council for Basic Education supported an educational view most similar to that of
   a. Admiral Hyman Rickover
   b. James B. Conant
   c. Mark Van Doren
   d. all of the above

9. Conant believed that the improvement of American public secondary education required
   a. fundamental changes in American schooling
   b. no radical changes in American secondary education
   c. elimination of vocational education programs
   d. all of the above

10. For Conant, the comprehensive high school
    a. developed a strong life-adjustment curriculum
    b. enrolled nearly all students in vocational education
    c. offered academic and vocational programs to respond to students' presumed intellectual abilities
    d. all of the above

11. In his emphasis on providing academic programs for "gifted" and "talented" youth, Conant
    a. separated himself from his contemporaries
    b. embraced a view commonly held by educational leaders at that time
    c. rejected the concept of meritocracy
    d. all of the above

12. "The divided world" concept was important to Conant because
    a. schools were to play an important role in competition with Soviet communism
    b. public awareness of "the divided world" would stimulate public support for schools
    c. it pointed to the importance of science and technology education
    d. all of the above

13. Conant believed that vocational education
    a. could be a tool for building unity between rich and poor
    b. was anti-democratic
    c. belonged in separate schools
    d. all of the above

14. In its approach to vocational education for African American students, Conant's advocacy of differentiated curricula resembled that of
    a. Charles Eliot
    b. John Collier
    c. Booker T. Washington
    d. all of the above

15. Conant advocated expansion of the junior college movement because it would contribute to
    a. social stability
    b. employable skills
    c. equal educational opportunity
    d. all of the above

16. In the authors' view, "national interest" was defined for Conant by
    a. what the majority of voters believed it to be
    b. what those in leadership positions believed it to be
    c. what schoolteachers believed it to be
    d. all of the above

17. The authors portray Conant's view of meritocracy as
    a. elitist
    b. democratic
    c. realistic
    d. all of the above

18. In "Education for All" Van Doren's educational views are most similar to those of
    a. Thomas Jefferson
    b. Charles Eliot
    c. Booker T. Washington
    d. all of the above

19. When Van Doren asks "how many men are capable of freedom," he implies agreement with
    a. Conant, who believed in meritocracy
    b. John Dewey, who believed in developmental democracy
    c. Admiral Rickover, who believed in a highly selective educational system
    d. all of the above

20. Van Doren believes individuals should be educated for
    a. citizenship
    b. democracy
    c. thinking well
    d. all of the above

21. When Van Doren calls for liberal and vocational education for all citizens, he seeks
    a. to prepare people for jobs
    b. equality of education
    c. comprehensive high schools
    d. all of the above

22. The "selective function" of schooling contributes to
    a. social stratification
    b. students receiving the kind of education best suited for them
    c. the democratization of education
    d. all of the above

23. Compared to the educational reforms of the progressive era, Conant's reforms can best be described as
    a. an extension of the earlier reforms
    b. a reversal of the earlier reforms
    c. not comparable to the earlier reforms
    d. all of the above

24. When Van Doren writes that the person should "be understood as an end, not a means," his idea is that
    a. people should be educated for specific social and political structures
    b. each person should be educated for his or her probable destiny in society
    c. the most human capacities of each person should be developed
    d. all of the above

25. Van Doren's opposition to education for social efficiency most resembles
    a. Booker T. Washington
    b. Charles Eliot
    c. Orestes Brownson
    d. all of the above

Answer Key

1. A	2. B	3. C	4. C	5. D
6. A	7. C	8. C	9. B	10. C
11. B	12. D	13. A	14. D	15. D
16. B	17. A	18. A	19. B	20. C
21. B	22. A	23. A	24. C	25. C

Chapter 8

Liberty and Literacy in the United States Today

CHAPTER OBJECTIVES

Among the objectives that Chapter 8 seeks to achieve are these:

1. Students are expected to deepen their understanding of the notion of literacy introduced in Chapter 2 and to use the concept "literacy" as a lens through which to view various perspectives on what it means to be educated.

2. Students should evaluate the degree to which four different perspectives on literacy--the conventional, the functional, the cultural, and the critical--can potentially serve different segments of society and different ideological orientations in different ways.

3. Students should evaluate the degree to which different literacy perspectives serve different educational goals.

4. Students should assess the degree to which Jefferson's conception of the connection between literacy and democracy may be best served by the critical literacy perspective and the degree to which the educational methods of critical pedagogy are necessary to achieve critical literacy.

5. Students should understand the basic tenets of cultural or ideological hegemony theory and evaluate the degree to which that theory is supported by data in this chapter and from their own experiences.

6. Students should assess the degree to which contemporary society is marked more by hegemonic than by participatory democratic processes, and the degree to which schools seem more successfully to serve one or the other of those two ideals.

CHAPTER OVERVIEW

Chapter 8 is the first chapter in Part II of the text and is thus the first chapter to develop Part I themes in a contemporary context. Chapter 8 seeks particularly to revisit the themes of liberty and literacy that are presented in Chapter 2. This chapter shows that the term "literacy" does not describe just one concept, but that what we mean by literacy changes with historical setting and with ideological orientation. What it was to be literate in Colonial times might not suffice, therefore, for what it means to be literate today. Judgments about a population's literacy thus depend upon what standard of literacy is being employed.

This chapter examines four different perspectives on literacy, each of which represents a different approach to thinking about what it means to be able to read and write in contemporary society. These four are: conventional literacy, functional literacy, cultural literacy, and critical literacy. These various perspectives on literacy are shown to be historically grounded in Jefferson's own respect for the importance of literacy in democratic life, for Jefferson's account of literacy shows partial affinities with each of these four perspectives. One issue that may be raised with each of these four approaches to literacy is the question of whose interests seem well served and whose interests seem poorly served by that particular approach. Classroom practices consistent with each approach to literacy are briefly examined, with particular attention to the pedagogical implications of critical literacy as developed by such educators as Paulo Freire, Donaldo Macedo, and Henry Giroux.

A fundamental obstacle to universal literacy as a direct route to intellectual and political liberty in the U. S., however, is the domination of cultural institutions and values by a relatively narrow range of ideological perspectives. The conventional, functional, and cultural literacies developed by American citizens may be said to fall short of a critical literacy that would allow most Americans to develop an alternative to the corporate liberal perspective that dominates American institutional leadership today. To interpret such phenomena, ideological or cultural hegemony theory is described and discussed. It would appear that mass media and the public schools play significant roles in maintaining the dominance of corporate liberal ideology in contemporary society. The Primary Source Reading at the end of the chapter shows how one contemporary educator seeks to foster critical literacy among his own students.

TEACHING SUGGESTIONS

1. Because most students have not experienced examples of the critical pedagogy described by William Bigelow in the Primary Source Reading, this selection is worth considerable discussion. For example, Bigelow's opening claim that "teaching should be partisan" can be interpreted in ways that may not be supportable in the public school. Students should be asked to evaluate, on the other hand, whether it is possible for teaching not to be partisan, particularly if cultural hegemony theory is supportable.

2. The concept of "hidden curriculum" is one that has become a standard part of the vocabulary of educators, but it is an unfamiliar term to most students. The relationship between the meaning of hidden curriculum and the role of schools in cultural hegemony is a valuable one to discuss. Bigelow's classroom approaches to writing and dialogue can be modeled as preservice teachers discuss their own experiences with hidden curriculum.

3. A theme of Part I of the book was that schools and teachers are ill-positioned to bring about significant social change, yet Bigelow seems to view his teaching as serving an agenda of social change. At the same time, he attempts to be realistic about what he can accomplish. Students can profitably be engaged in discussing whether Bigelow's approach is likely to make a difference in his students' lives, and why. What is the relationship of those possible differences to social change?

ESSAY QUESTIONS

Below are two kinds of essay questions:

   a. short essays or identification questions in which students are asked to write a descriptive paragraph or two to demonstrate their understanding of certain concepts, events, or practices; and

   b. longer essays, which allow students to demonstrate their ability to analyze more complex issues involving several events, concepts, and/or practices.

A. Identify and briefly indicate the significance of an assigned number of the following:
   a. conventional literacy
   b. functional literacy

      c. cultural literacy

      d. critical literacy

      e. Paulo Freire

      f. cultural hegemony

      g. mass media

      h. Organic Goodie Simulation

      i. teaching as a "subversive activity"

B. Write a well-ordered essay, 2-3 pages in length, in response to an assigned number of the following questions. Your essay, like the responses required of the questions at the end of each chapter of your text, requires you to take a position on a socio-educational issue and then defend that position with reasoned argument and evidence from the text and from other sources at your disposal. In each essay, you are expected to:

      a. clearly state your position or thesis;

      b. respond to *all parts* of the assigned question;

      c. defend your position with evidence and reasoned argument;

      d. demonstrate college-level writing skills.

1. How does cultural hegemony affect what happens in public school classrooms?

2. Explain the differences between functional, cultural, and critical literacy. Which kind of literacy should teachers aim for in public schools? Why?

3. Discuss how a teacher might approach the teaching of critical literacy. What groups might disapprove of such teaching? What should a teacher's response be to such groups?

MULTIPLE-CHOICE ITEMS

For each item, select the *best* answer from the four alternatives presented, as supported by your textbook. Students are encouraged to defend answers other than those in the answer key with evidence and argument, which may or may not prove compelling enough to have an alternate answer counted as correct.

1.   In order to understand use of the term "literacy rate," one of the things important to know is
   a. the political nature of the agency doing the survey
   b. the methods and definitions used to identify people as literate
   c. the literacy rates of other countries
   d. all of the above

2.   Today, a person who is illiterate is almost certain to have a greatly restricted social, economic, and political sphere of effective action. This is due largely to the fact that
   a. if one cannot read, it is difficult to come to an adequate understanding of political issues
   b. people who do not have at least a high school diploma find it difficult to get good-paying jobs
   c. in contemporary society, negative judgments are made about illiterate people, thus reducing their credibility and influence
   d. all of the above

3.   Literacy rates (whether conventional, functional, cultural, or critical literacy) can be influenced by
   a. access to the means of acquiring literacy
   b. social class
   c. gender
   d. all of the above

4.   The authors claim that "social differences in the meaning of literacy are crucial." An example of this concept is
   a. in a traditional, non-industrial society, literacy typically is just as highly valued for full social participation and status as in a modern post-industrial society
   b. the concept "literacy" may be used differently in different contexts to mean very different things, from ability to sign one's name to ability to follow complex written instructions
   c. literacy today may mean something very different for men than for women
   d. all of the above

5. The conventional literacy perspective may obscure systematic inequalities in which of the following?
   a. access to quality education
   b. family income
   c. different educational abilities
   d. all of the above

6. The authors indicate that economic class and functional illiteracy are related. An important causal factor for this relationship suggested in the text is that
   a. students from lower socioeconomic groups lack parental support for education
   b. students from middle- and upper-class families value education more than students from lower-class families do
   c. different socio-economic groups tend to receive different educations
   d. all of the above

7. An example of educational programming based on the functional literacy perspective might be
   a. SAT scores used as a basis for college admission
   b. pass/fail grading standards
   c. minimum competency testing
   d. all of the above

8. The functional literacy perspective is echoed in
   a. educational reform reports calling for the need for "an educated workforce"
   b. Jefferson's Virginia Plan
   c. Van Doren's "Education for All"
   d. all of the above

9. An important part of E.D. Hirsch's defense of his cultural literacy perspective is that it
   a. would enhance cultural pluralism in education
   b. emphasizes "thinking skills" over "memorization of facts"
   c. draws from the elements of culture shared by all groups in our society
   d. all of the above

10. Which of the following perspectives seems to embrace higher aspirations in the learner?
    a. conventional literacy
    b. functional literacy
    c. cultural literacy
    d. all of the above

11. An emphasis on teaching students how to think independently is importantly based on a desire for
    a. social stability
    b. social critique
    c. social mobility
    d. all of the above

12. The critical literacy perspective is aimed at
    a. strengthening public support for existing institutional arrangements
    b. overthrowing capitalism
    c. increasing public critique of social "givens"
    d. all of the above

13. Freire's conception of literacy would be most likely to view schooling as that which should
    a. emphasize citizenship education
    b. be geared towards minimizing cultural differences
    c. result in "thousands of one-man revolutions"
    d. all of the above

14. Critical literacy can be most closely aligned with the ideals of
    a. Mark Van Doren
    b. James B. Conant
    c. Horace Mann
    d. all of the above

15. Critical literacy can be judged to be effective to the extent it
    a. equips people to question unequal power relations effectively
    b. contributes to social stability
    c. overthrows the existing government
    d. all of the above

16. The authors claim that in our society, knowledge and power are interrelated. Evidence for this claim is that
    a. knowledge changes over time
    b. what "counts" as knowledge is determined by those in positions of influence in existing economic and social institutions
    c. what is important to know is debatable
    d. all of the above

17. The concept of "legitimating" students' knowledge and experience includes
    a. helping students learn to embrace the dominant ideology uncritically
    b. students coming to learn that other people share their understandings
    c. helping students see their own knowledge and experience as important for classroom discourse and study
    d. all of the above

18. Perhaps surprisingly, President Eisenhower's evaluation of the military-industrial complex might imply his support for education to be sympathetic to
    a. Conant's recommendations for more emphasis on science and math
    b. Freire's goals for literacy
    c. Hirsch's emphasis on culture
    d. all of the above

19. Elite theorists would be most likely to support education for
    a. critical literacy
    b. cultural literacy
    c. functional literacy
    d. all of the above

20. Critics who view the present educational system in the United States as being hegemonic would also be likely to
    a. make the same critique of the educational goals of the social efficiency progressives
    b. judge Freire's concept of critical literacy as hegemonic
    c. find E. D. Hirsch's "cultural literacy" to be emancipatory
    d. all of the above

21. The authors indicate that the dominant culture draws its power from
    a. processes of ideological and cultural hegemony
    b. the shared experiences of all social classes
    c. the informed consent of all voters
    d. all of the above

22. According to hegemony theorists, the stability of the U.S. social order can be attributed in part to
    a. an electorate without clear alternatives to the status quo
    b. citizen cooperation with hegemonic institutions
    c. the success of political socialization in schooling
    d. all of the above

23. According to hegemony theory, U.S. schooling is organized to
    a. contribute to educating students who understand and value the democratic ideals of participatory democracy
    b. serve students' interests in finding rewarding jobs
    c. contribute to developing decision-making abilities by those students who have been identified as possessing leadership qualities
    d. all of the above

24. In this chapter, what is termed "miseducation" can be applied to a person's
    a. failure to realize the existence and significance of unequal power relationships in the U.S.
    b. belief that his/her vote and/or participation cannot make a difference in social policy
    c. desire to act on behalf of what the national government has described as the national interest
    d. all of the above

25. William Bigelow's classroom effort to emphasize common experiences in the lives of his students was aimed at helping students
    a. discover to what extent their beliefs deviated from the norm
    b. find disparities between experience and rhetoric
    c. learn that individual experiences cannot be generalized to the wider society
    d. all of the above

26. Bigelow writes, "One function of the school curriculum is to celebrate the culture of the dominant." He hopes to make the point(s) that
    a. an appropriate curricular response to people whose culture is outside of the dominant culture would be recognition such as provided by Black History Month
    b. the culture shared by "the dominant" should be what is emphasized in the curriculum
    c. school curricula should be understood through, and recognize the importance of, the experiences of students
    d. all of the above

27. The hidden curriculum to which Bigelow refers might be illustrated in
    a. assigned classroom seating
    b. tracking
    c. multiple choice tests
    d. all of the above

28. Bigelow's "organic goodie simulation" was intended to demonstrate

    a. citizen cooperation, in the larger society, with hegemonic institutions

    b. that "the system" worked only because the students let it work

    c. the possibility of critical reflection and action against structures of oppression.

    d. all of the above

29. **Without** considering his further elaboration, Bigelow's assertion that teachers should be partisan might also been used to support

    a. teachers' favoring some students over others

    b. special opportunities for "gifted" students

    c. authoritarian classroom practices

    d. all of the above

Answer Key

1. B	2. D	3. D	4. B	5. A
6. C	7. C	8. A	9. C	10. C
11. B	12. C	13. C	14. A	15. A
16. B	17. C	18. B	19. B	20. A
21. A	22. D	23. C	24. D	25. B
26. C	27. D	28. D	29. D	

Chapter 9

Public School Teaching: A Gendered Profession

CHAPTER OBJECTIVES

Among the objectives that Chapter 9 seeks to achieve are these:

1. Students should reflect historically on the origins of teaching as an occupation and should critically evaluate the degree to which that occupation has become, is likely to become, and *should* become a profession.

2. Students should assess whether "professionalizing" teaching is likely to improve the quality of schooling, as its proponents claim.

3. Students should see that complete agreement does not exist on the definition of a profession and that there is room for interpretation on whether teaching is or is not a profession.

4. Students should become familiar with critical perspectives on the professionalization movement, particularly as these perspectives place gender in the forefront of their analysis.

5. Students should contrast the role gender plays in a critical analysis of professionalism against the role gender played in Horace Mann's conception of the feminization of teaching.

6. Students should evaluate whether Herbst's contrast of *professionalization* with *professionalism* is a useful one that can accommodate a critical analysis of gender.

CHAPTER OVERVIEW

Chapter 9 explores, with much different emphasis, two themes introduced in Chapter 3. The first is the improvement of public schooling through the improvement of teacher preparation, a concern which in contemporary discussions has become synonymous with "professionalization" of teaching. Second is the significance of gender in understanding the nature and status of teaching as an occupation. It was in Horace Mann's time that teaching became predominantly a female occupation, and today scholars are attaching new significance to gender in their efforts to understand that occupation.

After a brief history of teacher education in the United States is presented, the chapter focuses on the educational reform movement of the 1980s and 1990s. The importance of professionalization, standardization, and centralization of control in the teaching profession is examined in major school reform reports of the 1980s. The chapter questions of the degree to which the term "profession" currently applies to teaching and, later, questions whether teaching can or should be a profession with the trappings of other established professions.

To answer these two questions, the chapter develops a "critical perspective" on teaching as a profession. This critical perspective examines issues of low pay, lack of control over workplace decisions, and the predominance of women in teaching as these conditions interact with one another to influence the status and rewards in teaching. This analysis suggests that "professionalization" of teaching appears to be a solution proposed and imposed by educational reformers other than teachers themselves and is symptomatic of the lack of control of teachers over the conditions of their occupation. The chapter suggests that by remaining "gender-neutral," reformers who propose professionalization are failing to support teachers' efforts to examine their own occupational problems and to devise and implement their own solutions. This chapter concludes by reviewing current data on the status and rewards of the teaching occupation, issues that appear to be central in the Primary Source Reading, a published dialogue between a veteran and beginning teacher.

TEACHING SUGGESTIONS

1. A number of themes from the chapter have to do with the conditions of teaching, its autonomy and its rewards. Students sensitive to these themes can find them made concrete in the dialogue between Clare Fox and Margaret Metzger (the spelling in the textbook is erroneous). Students can become discouraged by the negative dimensions of teaching portrayed in this dialogue, and they should be asked to discuss those negative dimensions and how teachers might overcome them. In

particular, students might be referred back to Bigelow's claim that teachers need to work together in groups to support one another.

2. Students can relate this Primary Source Reading to the central issues in the chapter also by evaluating whether the professionalization movement is likely to address the problems discussed by Metzger and Fox. As part of this discussion, students can offer their own ideas for how Metzger's and Fox's problems might best be resolved, and whether these solutions require "professionalization."

3. Finally, students should be engaged in discussing whether gender plays a role in the Metzger-Fox dialogue and whether that dialogue would likely be just the same if it were being held by two males.

ESSAY QUESTIONS

Below are two kinds of essay questions:

    a. short essays or identification questions in which students are asked to write a descriptive paragraph or two to demonstrate their understanding of certain concepts, events, or practices; and

    b. longer essays, which allow students to demonstrate their ability to analyze more complex issues involving several events, concepts, and/or practices.

A. Identify and briefly indicate the significance of an assigned number of the following:
    a. profession
    b. managed occupation
    c. expert management
    d. Holmes Report
    e. professionalization
    f. professionalism
    g. *Metropolitan Life Survey of the American Teacher*

B. Write a well-ordered essay, 2-3 pages in length, in response to an assigned number of the following questions. Your essay, like the responses required of the questions at the end of each chapter of your text, requires you to take a position on a socio-educational issue and then defend that position with reasoned argument and evidence from the text and from other sources at your disposal. In each essay, you are expected to:

a. clearly state your position or thesis;

b. respond to *all parts* of the assigned question;

c. defend your position with evidence and reasoned argument;

d. demonstrate college-level writing skills.

1. Some educational theorists have argued that making teaching a"profession" will solve many of the problems with American public schools. Explain why some defend this position, and evaluate the counterarguments to it.

2. Explain how the current management structure of American public schools contributes to teacher dissatisfaction. How might this situation be improved?

3. Discuss whether it is really important, in your view, to consider gender in an analysis of the effectiveness of teachers in public schools today. In your analysis, consider whether gender is significant for understanding teacher autonomy, teacher rewards, public support for schooling, and other dimensions that might have a bearing on the effectiveness of schools.

MULTIPLE-CHOICE ITEMS

For each item, select the *best* answer from the four alternatives presented, as supported by your textbook. Students are encouraged to defend answers other than those in the answer key with evidence and argument, which may or may not prove compelling enough to have an alternate answer counted as correct.

1. The most important commonality underlying the teacher professionalization movements of Horace Mann's time and today is

a. the need to raise teachers' salaries

b. the desire to make teaching as prestigious as law or medicine

c. the intention to improve schooling

d. all of the above

2. Horace Mann's normal schools helped to
    a. pull together a specialized body of teaching knowledge
    b. make teaching a more female-occupied profession
    c. standardize the quality and content of schooling
    d. all of the above

3. As the normal school era drew to an end, the professionalization of teaching and the professionalization of school administration
    a. created tension regarding the autonomy of teachers
    b. elevated the status of colleges of education
    c. clearly improved the quality of schooling
    d. all of the above

4. James B. Conant's efforts to professionalize teaching
    a. created greater autonomy for teachers
    b. emphasized the teacher's right to determine his or her own professional tasks in the classroom
    c. did not appear to accomplish their goals
    d. all of the above

5. In *Tomorrow's Teachers*, the Holmes Group sought to
    a. reject comparisons among teaching and medicine and law
    b. reject a professionalization model for teaching
    c. improve the quality of schooling by improving the education of teachers
    d. all of the above

6. Efforts at centralizing control of teaching standards were characteristic of
    a. Horace Mann's common school movement
    b. the Holmes Group's *Tomorrow's Teachers*
    c. the Carnegie Forum's Task Force on Teaching as a Profession
    d. all of the above

7. John Goodlad believes teaching is a "weak" profession mostly because
    a. its status and prestige do not compare well to other professions
    b. the professional knowledge base in teaching is inadequate
    c. the nature of the work in teaching is not predominantly intellectual
    d. all of the above

8. Although teaching does not seem to compare well to other professions in terms of status, material rewards, or a codified body of specialized knowledge, it may still qualify as a profession because
   a. it embodies a moral vision and commitment regarding human society
   b. at least teachers have professional autonomy
   c. it attracts college students who are academically stronger than most other college students
   d. all of the above

9. Critics of proposals for career ladders in teaching are concerned
   a. that professional autonomy would be reserved only for those at the top of the career ladder
   b. that the most successful teachers would spend the least time in the classroom
   c. that such proposals do not address the fundamental problems of the teaching profession that reside in the wider society
   d. all of the above

10. Dee Ann Spencer's assessment of teaching as a quasi-profession
    a. contradicts Goodlad's assessment of teaching
    b. recognizes the issue of gender as significant to professional status
    c. contradicts the Carnegie Forum's satisfaction with the teaching profession
    d. all of the above

11. Geraldine Clifford claims that teaching is an underpaid profession
    a. as a result of twentieth century industrialization
    b. largely due to the fact that teaching is a "feminine" profession
    c. in part due to the low social status of children
    d. all of the above

12. The textbook authors appear to believe that a central reason for low pay in teaching is
    a. cost of living differences in different states
    b. the influence of gender differences in occupations
    c. poor preparation of teachers in institutions of higher education
    d. all of the above

13. Most fundamental decisions affecting the conditions of teaching are made primarily by
    a. a wide variety of different agencies and institutions
    b. teachers and teachers' unions
    c. state governments
    d. all of the above

14. Casey and Apple argue that the best way to conceive of the teacher's role is "woman as teacher" because
    a. this conception offers the surest and most direct route to true professionalization for teachers
    b. this portrayal directs attention to women's perceptions of their occupational needs and aspirations
    c. this conception grants administrative positions to males and females in equal proportion
    d. all of the above

15. Like Casey and Apple, Susan Laird's analysis of the teaching profession
    a. does not assume that professionalization is a necessary approach to improving the quality of teaching and schooling
    b. offers a route to professionalization that is "gender neutral," because gender should be irrelevant to the quality of teaching
    c. recognizes that women are distinctively well suited for teaching because of their nurturing dispositions
    d. all of the above

16. The occupation of teaching is underpaid in part because, in the authors' view,
    a. state and local tax dollars have not been raised as much as they should be
    b. the nation must remain committed to other priorities such as defense spending
    c. the dominant ideology in contemporary society does not foster full discussion of possibilities for funding schooling
    d. all of the above

17. Herbst's contrast between *professionalization* and *professionalism*
    a. rejects the comparison between teaching and other professions
    b. questions credentialing and career ladders as useful ways of improving schooling
    c. values teachers' determining their own occupational structure
    d. all of the above

18. According to recent survey data, most teachers
    a. expect to leave the profession within the next five years
    b. intend to stay in the profession for many years to come
    c. hope to be administrators someday
    d. all of the above

19. Studies of what teachers find professionally satisfying report
    a. factors that seem to apply to other occupations, also
    b. that salary remains a highly significant factor
    c. factors such as autonomy, creativity, and opportunity for professional growth
    d. all of the above

20. As public school classrooms become increasingly comprised of African-American and Latino populations
    a. the percentage of minority teachers is increasing, also
    b. increasing numbers of new teachers seek to teach in inner cities
    c. the high percentage of Caucasian teachers presents a challenge to the teaching profession
    d. all of the above

21. The authors appear to believe that
    a. there is reason to be skeptical about professionalization as the "cure" for what ails public schooling
    b. teacher training is less important than good subject matter knowledge
    c. teacher shortages justify "alternative certification" programs
    d. all of the above

22. The authors appear to believe that
    a. the historical feminization of teaching may be a strength rather than a weakness in the effort to improve schooling
    b. the historical feminization of teaching may be a long-term obstacle to equalizing status and rewards between teaching and other professions
    c. a crucial goal for teachers should be professional autonomy in the context of professional responsibility to many constituencies
    d. all of the above

23. In Clare Fox's first letter, her mother's concerns about Clare's becoming a teacher probably reflect a concern about the
    a. sincerity of Clare's desire to be a teacher
    b. low status and rewards of teaching
    c. tight job market in teaching
    d. all of the above

24. Despite her evident satisfaction in teaching, Margaret Metzger is unhappy with her job because
    a. the routines become monotonous
    b. the quality of her work is not reflected in her pay
    c. it is physically draining
    d. all of the above

25. Despite the frustrations, Margaret Metzger's evaluation of her job is that
    a. she continues to grow professionally and intellectually
    b. a nurturing occupation is rewarding for her
    c. the satisfaction outweighs the frustrations
    d. all of the above

ANSWER KEY

1. C	2. D	3. A	4. C	5. C
6. D	7. B	8. A	9. D	10. B
11. C	12. B	13. A	14. B	15. A
16. C	17. D	18. B	19. D	20. C
21. A	22. D	23. B	24. D	25. D

Chapter 10

Schooling and Social Inequality: Race, Gender, and Class

CHAPTER OBJECTIVES

Among the objectives that Chapter 10 seeks to achieve are these:

1. Students should question the basic educational assumption that school success is based primarily or even largely on children's capacity for learning.

2. In investigating other variables that might influence school learning, students should evaluate the degree to which race, ethnicity, social class, and gender influence outcomes.

3. Students should evaluate the limitations of the emphasis that liberal ideology places on individual responsibility for school success and should question whether a "neutral" treatment of all students is genuinely equitable.

4. Students should discuss how the political economic context of schooling influences student outcomes, which in turn influence economic opportunities, which in turn influence student outcomes for a new generation.

5. Students should compare and contrast the primary principles of different theories of social inequality and should evaluate which of these seems best to explain the data available in this chapter.

6. Students should assess the degree to which the concept of "gender-sensitive" schooling can be modified to race- and ethnicity-sensitivity to respond to the needs of students from different ethnic and social class backgrounds.

CHAPTER OVERVIEW

Chapter 10 corresponds to Chapters 4 and 6 in its emphasis on race and ethnicity and attends also to gender as an element of social and educational inequity. The prevailing themes of this chapter are: first, what issues to take into account when thinking about social and educational policies that are equitable for all ethnic and gender groups, and second, what implications such thinking might have for educational policies and classroom processes. The chapter begins by reviewing the history of efforts to address educational equity since the 1954 Brown vs. Board of Education of Topeka, Kansas decision and focuses particularly on the current indicators of political- economic inequality in American culture. For different ethnic and gender groups, such categories as income, employment, family status, housing, and political power are examined.

The chapter then turns away from these social inequalities to examine contemporary scholarship on the relations between education and inequality for various ethnic, economic, and gender groups. In considering these data, competing theories of social inequality are presented. These include: genetic deficit theory, cultural deficit theory, and critical theory, which incorporates cultural difference theory, cultural subordination theory, and resistance theory in the general effort to explain the nature of educational and social inequality in the United States.

Finally, the chapter turns to a variety of pedagogical approaches to supporting students of different ethnicities and gender in the classroom. A "gender-sensitive" approach is presented as a model for teachers who seek to be sensitive to cultural and gender differences and who at the same time seek to equip their students to succeed by the standards of the dominant society. Various approaches to "multicultural education" are examined and two educational programs are presented as examples of "programs that work" with diverse students. The need for teachers to take a broader view of the diversity of student capacities for learning is emphasized in the Primary Source Reading in which an American Indian father urges a teacher to understand the distinctive abilities of his kindergarten-age son. The boy is not, as the father reminds the teacher, culturally "disadvantaged," but culturally "different," with impressive achievements of his own.

TEACHING SUGGESTIONS

1. The Primary Source Reading by Robert Lake can be a provocative one in helping students see that the intelligence of children from some cultural backgrounds may go unrewarded in the standard public school classroom. Students should evaluate whether Lake's claim that his son is "caught between two worlds, torn by two distinct cultural systems" is relevant for understanding the performance of Asian-American, African-American, Latino, and other cultural groups in schools.

2. The question of gender difference in school experiences is one on which students tend to be quite divided. Many preservice teachers are women and a significant number of them have had largely successful experiences in schools. Some of them are therefore resistant to the view that the classroom climate of schools is any different for girls than for boys. A significant question to raise, however, is whether that perceived lack of difference is true for girls of lower socioeconomic backgrounds and for girls from minority ethnic groups.

3. One distinctive feature of this textbook is the degree to which issues of gender and ethnicity pervade the historical as well as the contemporary portrayals of schooling in the United States. Faculty can now drawn upon the intellectual capital developed in the students through their encounters with the Irish, southern and eastern Europeans, African-Americans, and American Indians in Part I of the text as they raise questions about the pervasiveness of race and gender as significant variables in understanding American schools and American society.

ESSAY QUESTIONS

Below are two kinds of essay questions:

   a. short essays or identification questions in which students are asked to write a descriptive paragraph or two to demonstrate their understanding of certain concepts, events, or practices; and

   b. longer essays, which allow students to demonstrate their ability to analyze more complex issues involving several events, concepts, and/or practices.

A. Identify and briefly indicate the significance of an assigned number of the following:

    a. G.I. Bill

    b. Coleman Report

    c. cultural deprivation studies

    d Jane Elliott's experiment

    e. Scholastic Achievement Tests

    f. socioeconomic class

    g. genetic inferiority theory

    h. cultural deficit theory

    i. cultural difference theory

    j. cultural subordination theory

    k. resistance theory

    l. multicultural education

B. Write a well-ordered essay, 2-3 pages in length, in response to an assigned number of the following questions. Your essay, like the responses required of the questions at the end of each chapter of your text, requires you to take a position on a socio-educational issue and then defend that position with reasoned argument and evidence from the text and from other sources at your disposal. In each essay, you are expected to:

    a. clearly state your position or thesis;

    b. respond to *all parts* of the assigned question;

    c. defend your position with evidence and reasoned argument;

    d. demonstrate college-level writing skills.

1. A basic assumption underlying American schooling has been that students' success in schools and in economic life is based on their own learning abilities in an equitable educational system. Critically analyze this assumption.

2. The Coleman Report was a major document in the post World War II American schooling debates. Critically analyze the Report and the response to it by modern liberals (e.g., Daniel Patrick Moynihan and Christopher Jencks).

3. What are the lessons prospective teacher might learn from Jane Elliott's experiment? How are these important to the effectiveness of the teacher, in your view?

4. What role has gender played in the ways Americans have organized and conducted schooling? Does your own experience tend to confirm or disconfirm the portrayal of gendered education in this chapter? Explain.

MULTIPLE-CHOICE ITEMS

For each item, select the *best* answer from the four alternatives presented, as supported by your textbook. Students are encouraged to defend answers other than those in the answer key with evidence and argument, which may or may not prove compelling enough to have an alternate answer counted as correct.

1. Social theorists who characterize the U.S. economic structure as meritocratic would be likely to disagree with which of the following?
    a. Race and gender tend to be as influential as talent and hard work in determining who succeeds in society
    b. While social inequality always will exist, the free market system at least allows all people an equal chance to get ahead based on talent and hard work
    c. The school system, at least, rewards talent and hard work without regard to race, gender, or economic status
    d. all of the above

2. The authors state that "the privileged often find it comforting as well as expedient to interpret...socially derived inequalities as intrinsic personal qualities." This can be seen in practices such as
    a. intramural athletics
    b. tracking or ability-grouping
    c. cooperative learning
    d. all of the above

3. Which of these best characterizes the meaning of "meritocracy?"
    a. those with talent and hard work will get ahead
    b. government by the wealthy
    c. democracies should provide equality of educational opportunity
    d. all of the above

4. Advocates of a meritocratic arrangement for society claim that differentiated curricula are fair because
   a. mixed "ability grouping" has been shown to be effective
   b. they allow each student to work to the best of his or her ability
   c. schools should not be in the business of preparing students for jobs
   d. all of the above

5. Confusing culturally diverse traits with character or behavior deficiencies can be one of the hallmarks of
   a. meritocracy
   b. pluralism
   c. ethnocentrism
   d. all of the above

6. Identifying the problems experienced by marginalized groups as deficiencies in individuals, rather than connecting the problems to their cultural histories, provides justification for
   a. differentiated curricula
   b. ability grouping
   c. vocational education
   d. all of the above

7. Which of the following is characteristic of education for maintaining a meritocratic social order?
   a. equal educational opportunity to acquire the education for which one is best suited
   b. the assumption that educational achievement will prevent someone from being marginalized
   c. tracking or ability grouping
   d. all of the above

8. According to the authors, the college successes of individuals who took advantage of the GI Bill had the potential to challenge the ideology of meritocracy. However, this potential was largely unrealized because

    a. these successful students learned to adopt meritocratic ideals themselves
    b. the GI Bill students went back into the working classes and were silenced
    c. not very many GI Bill students actually succeeded in college
    d. all of the above

9. The belief that it is unreasonable to expect schooling to bring about significant academic gains in most students is reinforced by

    a. Coleman's data showing that educational inputs make little difference in student achievement
    b. research showing the inherent differences in children's readiness for school
    c. equating lack of opportunity for learning with lack of intelligence
    d. all of the above

10. "Cultural deprivation" theories have significantly contributed to

    a. directing attention away from the role of structured social inequalities in producing differences among students
    b. focusing curricular development in multicultural education
    c. increasing curricular attention to a variety of teaching and learning styles in teacher education programs
    d. all of the above

11. According to the authors, wealth and power have a positive correlation in U.S. society. If this statement reflects the reality of the experiences of Americans, then

    a. the extent to which the democratic principle of equality is being realized in our society must be questioned
    b. education should focus primarily on career skills so that people can find better-paying jobs
    c. more emphasis needs to be placed on equal educational opportunity
    d. all of the above

12. Which of the following is(are) consistent with the concept of equal educational opportunity?

    a. differentiated curriculum

    b. tracking and ability grouping

    c. SAT and ACT testing

    d. all of the above

13. Correlating with the myth that IQ scores measure a general capacity to learn is(are) the assumption(s) that

    a. intelligence is largely a genetic capacity

    b. the SAT is a reliable indicator of intellectual abilities

    c. one's socioeconomic status is primarily based on one's willingness to work

    d. all of the above

14. Compensatory education programs are consistent with

    a. classical liberalism

    b. the cultural literacy perspective

    c. cultural deficiency theory

    d. all of the above

15. The evidence presented in this chapter in support for the claim that schools participate in the subordination of certain groups based on race, ethnicity, class and gender includes:

    a. the schools' devaluation of Black English Vernacular and of those who speak it

    b. correlations between SAT scores and family income

    c. examples of programs that succeed academically with students who would typically be expected to perform poorly

    d. all of the above

16. Focusing primarily on the aspects of culture which <u>are</u> shared by students from diverse backgrounds is likely to be

    a. a pluralist approach

    b. an assimilationist approach

    c. a reconstructionist approach

    d. all of the above

17. Which of these could reasonably be described as demonstrating an important connection between cultural deficit theory and teacher perceptions?

    a. generally lower rate of school success for BEV speakers than for Standard English speakers

    b. Cubans have a higher family income level than African Americans, and generally also have a higher rate of school success

    c. Korean students tend to perform as poorly, relatively, in Japanese schools as African American students perform in U.S. schools

    d. all of the above

18. The fact that low-income African Americans have lower school success rates than white Americans is

    a. proof that African Americans cannot meet the demands of schooling

    b. a result of lack of home- or peer group-support for achievement in school

    c. often partly a result of a relationship that arises from the interaction of BEV and the school

    d. all of the above

19. Some societal expectations, including expectations teachers have regarding students, turn out to be self-fulfilling prophecies. In light of this, a reasonable argument can be made for which of the following?

    a. teacher expectations are the primary cause of academic failure

    b. schooling is very successful in teaching social norms

    c. regardless of income level, the probability of entering college after completing high school is lower for girls than for boys

    d. all of the above

20. A potential problem with the view that, if we "treat each student as an individual" we do not have to be concerned about the race, ethnicity or gender of the child, is that

    a. different racial groups need different curricula

    b. in important ways, each child's individual identity is partly formed by race, ethnicity, and gender, and recognizing each child as an individual requires understanding how those components help shape the individual

    c. boys and girls inherently have different levels of academic ability

    d. all of the above

21. Jane Elliott's Discrimination Day experiment was a powerful example of
    a. the social construction of inferiority and superiority
    b. how social construction of differences among people can be hurtful
    c. how easily group membership can lead people to discriminate against one another
    d. all of the above

22. Following the Supreme Court decision in *Brown v. Board of Education*, legal desegregation has had demonstrable success in
    a. institutions of higher learning
    b. public schools
    c. government office-holding
    d. all of the above

23. An important contribution that feminist theory has made to interpreting the relationship between gender and education has been
    a. an increase in curricular attention to the social worth of values traditionally viewed as being "feminine"
    b. a significant increase in the percentage of males entering the teaching profession
    c. equalization of numbers of women and men in educational administration and college professorships
    d. all of the above

24. Parents of upper- and middle-class socioeconomic status are more likely than parents of lower-class standing to participate actively in their children's formal schooling. This is, in part, an important reflection of
    a. the lack of desire among lower SES parents for their children to succeed
    b. the similarities between schools and upper middle-class families in terms of language, values, and customs
    c. the fact that upper-middle-class people tend to have time on their hands
    d. all of the above

25. When a child is having trouble in school, one way to look for possible sources for the trouble is to identify areas of "fit" or "mismatch" between the school culture and the child's culture. This method characterizes
    a. critical theory
    b. cultural deficit theory
    c. equity theory
    d. all of the above

26. E.D. Hirsch's delineation of the necessary components of cultural literacy reflects
    a. the classical view of education
    b. the modern liberal view of education
    c. the critical theorists' view of education
    d. all of the above

27. One of the primary functions of education is to bring the youth of society into the culture of that society. Depending on how "culture" has been defined and reflected in educational policies, various critics have claimed that
    a. schooling contributes to perpetuating social inequalities
    b. schooling has resulted in cultural "illiterates"
    c. schooling prepares students for their eventual positions in the labor market
    d. all of the above

ANSWER KEY

1. A	2. B	3. A	4. B	5. C
6. A	7. D	8. A	9. D	10. A
11. A	12. D	13. D	14. C	15. D
16. D	17. D	18. C	19. C	20. B
21. D	22. D	23. A	24. B	25. A
26. B	27. D			

Chapter 11

Vocational and Liberal Education Today

CHAPTER OBJECTIVES

Among the objectives that Chapter 11 seeks to achieve are these:

1. This chapter is intended to deepen and extend the challenge, developed in Chapters 4 and 5, to the vocationalist educational thinking that tends to frame the importance of schooling in terms of preparation for earning an income.

2. Students should assess the extent to which the arguments for vocational education in public schools are supportable. They should also question whether vocational education seems to serve poorly the very portions of the population it is intended to serve well.

3. Students should evaluate the rhetoric of vocational education advocates in contrast to available data on the actual nature of the American workplace in the foreseeable future.

4. Students should evaluate whether a revised view of vocational education, one that focuses on traditionally liberal educational goals instead of preparation for the workplace, may be more supportable for educational and economic reasons.

5. Students should develop a critical appreciation of the historical ideal of liberal education and should consider ways in which that ideal could be used to serve the interests of all students in schools.

6. Students should examine the potential of liberal education for embodying democratic ideals in education more thoroughly than a vocationalist or differentiated-curriculum approach.

CHAPTER OVERVIEW

Chapter 11 is significant to the book as a whole in two distinctive ways. First, it corresponds to Chapter 5 in its attention to the contrast between vocational and liberal ideals in education. Second, it makes explicit a theme that has pervaded the volume up to this point: while the historic ideals of liberal education have come to us from cultures that were racist, sexist, and class-biased, the emphasis of these ideals on the full development of the intellectual and emotional capacities of each person, and the idea that as human beings we have more in common than in contrast with one another regarding these capacities, are worthy of shaping our educational aims for all students, regardless of race, ethnicity, social class or gender. It is the contention of this chapter that the historic development of vocational education goals, programs, and results has not served the democratic ideal of "the all-around growth of every member of society" that Dewey advocated and that remains compelling today. While the most recent vocational education manifesto examined in this chapter is *The Unfinished Agenda: The Role of Vocational Education in the High School* (1984), it is important for students to recognize that arguments for vocational education programs in public schools have continued to recur throughout the twentieth century and will likely continue into the next century as well. *The Unfinished Agenda* restates many of the arguments that have sustained vocational education throughout the twentieth century. This chapter, however, contends that the vocationalist arguments do not well serve the full development of the students in vocational educational programs, nor the economy of the United States. The chapter examines current data on the nature of the job market, its fastest-growing occupations, and the conditions of labor today in an effort to question the basic arguments recurrently put forward in support of vocational education programs in public schools.

The chapter then turns to examining a different approach to vocational education, one that uses vocational methods to achieve traditionally liberal education ideals. Examples of current practice are given to support this Deweyan approach to education *through* vocations instead of education *for* vocations. So that students can better understand what is meant by a "liberal education ideal," a brief history of the concept of liberal education is presented, reaching from Aristotle to Jane Roland Martin's feminist critique of the liberal education ideal. The idea that our best educational ideals should be held up for all of our students, not just the "academically inclined," is explored by secondary school teacher John Duffy in the Primary Source Reading at the chapter's end. Duffy rejects both ability grouping and vocational education in his effort to incorporate a "critical pedagogy" that stimulates the intellectual capacities of all of his students.

TEACHING SUGGESTIONS

1. This chapter taps into vocationalist critiques in Chapters 4, 5, and 7, and these connections should be made explicit for students through classroom dialogue and writing. While that critique constitutes a significant part of this chapter, equally significant is the relatively clear and concise account of the nature and value of a liberal education. It is a term about which students tend to have heard much and thought little. This chapter offers an occasion for them to think about how well their own education has lived up to an ideal of liberal education that they might construct and endorse.

2. It may be necessary to emphasize to students that the contrast between vocational education and liberal education is not so simple as anti-intellectual vs. intellectual, or anti-democratic vs. democratic. Students should see that the liberal education ideal has embraced its own forms of racism, class bias, and sexism, just as vocational education has worked against the interests of the working class, women, and people of color. This chapter suggests reconstructing the use of vocational education, and the ideal and practice of liberal education.

3. John Duffy's article, "Getting Off Track," undermines a central component of the vocational education tradition, namely, ability grouping. In doing so, Duffy embraces a model of critical pedagogy that can illustrate to preservice teachers the appropriateness of challenging academic work for students of all skill levels. Preservice teachers should be engaged in assessing the worth of Duffy's approach as a contemporary way to embrace liberal education ideals for all students.

ESSAY QUESTIONS

Below are two kinds of essay questions:

a. short essays or identification questions in which students are asked to write a descriptive paragraph or two to demonstrate their understanding of certain concepts, events, or practices; and

b. longer essays, which allow students to demonstrate their ability to analyze more complex issues involving several events, concepts, and/or practices.

A. Identify and briefly indicate the significance of an assigned number of the following:
   a. critical education
   b. banking education
   c. vocational education
   d. *Vocational Education and Training: Impact on Youth*
   e. liberal education
   f. *Unfinished Agenda: the Role of Vocational Education in the High School*
   g. *Carl D. Perkins Vocational and Applied Technological Education Act*
   h. "False Promises of Community Colleges"
   i. *General Education in a Free Society*

B. Write a well-ordered essay, 2-3 pages in length, in response to an assigned number of the following questions. Your essay, like the responses required of the questions at the end of each chapter of your text, requires you to take a position on a socio-educational issue and then defend that position with reasoned argument and evidence from the text and from other sources at your disposal. In each essay, you are expected to:
   a. clearly state your position or thesis;
   b. respond to *all parts* of the assigned question;
   c. defend your position with evidence and reasoned argument;
   d. demonstrate college-level writing skills.

1. Vocational educators often cite John Dewey's ideas as the foundation of the philosophy of vocational education. Critically examine this claim.

2. Explain why the works of John Grasso and John Shea, Fred Pincus and Arthur Wirth undermine the rationale for vocational education.

3. Examine the major differences in the aims of vocational education and liberal education. Which seems most appropriate in modern America, in terms of both economic efficiency and individual fulfillment?

4. Vocational education has always assumed some kind of "tracking" as the basis upon which vocational programs would be built. Discuss this assumption in light of the arguments of John Duffy.

MULTIPLE-CHOICE ITEMS

For each item, select the *best* answer from the four alternatives presented, as supported by your textbook. Students are encouraged to defend answers other than those in the answer key with evidence and argument, which may or may not prove compelling enough to have an alternate answer counted as correct.

1. James B. Conant's approach to vocational education in the 1960s
    a. captured the true spirit of John Dewey's educational thought
    b. was integral to his conception of the comprehensive high school
    c. sought to restore the Classical educational heritage for all students
    d. all of the above

2. Career education
    a. was based on basic premises similar to those of the vocational education movement of the Progressive era
    b. successfully replaced vocational education in most secondary school curricula
    c. was a major turn away from vocationalist reasoning
    d. all of the above

3.   Vocational education in secondary schools

    a.   is largely a twentieth century phenomenon in the U.S.

    b.   appears to be on the rise in popularity

    c.   appears to be decreasing in emphasis in recent years

    d.   all of the above

4.   The goals of vocational education programs

    a.   are similar to those embraced by Mark Van Doren

    b.   would be embraced by most upper middle class parents for their children

    c.   have remained basically intact in the twentieth century

    d.   all of the above

5.   In the 1970s and 1980s research findings indicated that secondary school vocational education

    a.   had mixed results in combatting high school dropout rates

    b.   did not appear to contribute to a greater likelihood of post-secondary schooling

    c.   has not been well matched to specific needs of the labor market

    d.   all of the above

6.   Research seems to indicate that general literacy skills

    a.   are a significant contributor to workers' success in the labor market

    b.   are not as important in getting employment as specific vocational skills

    c.   are desirable, but they won't help you get a job

    d.   all of the above

7.   The community college system may be characterized as

    a.   a true embodiment of equality of educational opportunity for all

    b.   an extension of the vocational education movement in the twentieth century

    c.   simply a trade school system

    d.   all of the above

8. A significant number of students enroll in community colleges so they may transfer to four-year colleges,
   a. and most of them succeed in doing so
   b. but only a small percentage of these students ever receive a baccalaureate degree
   c. but four-year colleges are not interested in transfer students
   d. all of the above

9. The relationships between community colleges, the workplace, and four-year baccalaureate institutions
   a. work effectively to help most community students obtain baccalaureate degrees
   b. are clearly and accurately described in community college handbooks
   c. may not be clearly understood by community college students themselves
   d. all of the above

10. In terms of total numbers of new jobs available, the fastest growing occupations in the late 1980s were *not*
    a. industrial production jobs
    b. related to high technology
    c. jobs that require a college degree
    d. all of the above

11. In terms of total numbers of new jobs available, the fastest growing occupations in the late 1980s were
    a. largely low-skill, low-paying jobs
    b. mostly in the service sector
    c. jobs with little career advancement opportunity
    d. all of the above

12. Workforce competency reports conducted in recent years do *not* suggest
    a. general literacy skills are little valued by most employers
    b. problem solving skills are little valued by most employers
    c. more time should be devoted to specific job preparation in secondary schools
    d. all of the above

13. The greatest agreement among workforce competency reports appears to be that employers value most in prospective employees
    a. literacy skills
    b. mathematical skills
    c. problem solving and decision-making skills
    d. all of the above

14. Most women in the workforce today
    a. have significantly lower incomes than men in similar positions
    b. are working in clerical and service occupations
    c. are not working in managerial or professional occupations
    d. all of the above

15. In terms of family income, the 1980s
    a. witnessed a widening of the gap between white and black families
    b. brought a closing of the gap between white and black families
    c. left most families better off than they were a decade earlier
    d. all of the above

16. Black unemployment tends to stay about twice as high as white unemployment,
    a. even among well-educated African-Americans
    b. except in times when the economy is doing well overall
    c. because African-Americans do not value education as much as Euro-Americans do
    d. all of the above

17. One of the key contributors to job satisfaction appears to be
    a. opportunity for significant input into decisions that affect one's work
    b. opportunity for creativity
    c. interest in the work itself
    d. all of the above

18. John Dewey's respect for school shops, laboratories, and occupational activities
    a. was successfully embodied in Progressive Era vocational education programs
    b. did not reflect a belief in education for the workplace
    c. had little or nothing to do with his respect for academic achievement
    d. all of the above

19. The Foxfire curriculum of cultural journalism and the 4-H programs of rural America might be regarded as examples of
    a. career education
    b. education for the workplace
    c. education through vocations
    d. all of the above

20. A primary ingredient in Jefferson's and Aristotle's regard for liberal education was the relationship between
    a. masculinity and elitism
    b. wealth and aristocracy
    c. rationality and freedom
    d. all of the above

21. Historically, liberal education tends to emphasize
    a. both breadth and depth of study
    b. preparation for the world of work
    c. general learning without specialization
    d. all of the above

22. The Yale report of 1828 might be said to embody faculty psychology because
    a. it was written by the faculty of Yale University
    b. it employs the metaphors of mind as a muscle and mind as a container or room to be filled
    c. it taxes one's faculties to understand it
    d. all of the above

23. The authors of this volume appear to believe that the ideal of liberal education
    a. should be rejected because of its inherent racism
    b. should be rejected because of its inherent elitism
    c. can be reconceptualized to correct for historic racist and sexist tendencies
    d. all of the above

24. Feminist author Jane Roland Martin criticizes traditional conceptions of liberal education because
    a. they are basically elitist
    b. they are so vague and murky that no one can agree on what liberal education means
    c. they pay insufficient attention to the full range of emotional, logical and other human capacities shared by both men and women
    d. all of the above

25. The authors of this volume appear to believe that a reconceptualized liberal education can be an appropriate ideal
    a. for all students throughout their elementary and secondary schooling
    b. but that it really wouldn't be liberal education anymore
    c. for males, but not necessarily females
    d. all of the above

26. In "Getting Off Track," teacher John Duffy argues that ability grouping or "tracking"
    a. is an effective way for teachers to reach all students at their own skill levels
    b. is inconsistent with critical pedagogy
    c. allows students to grow in self esteem because they won't be compared to students more skillful than they
    d. all of the above

27. Duffy's conception of critical pedagogy is illustrated, he believes, by
    a. a variety of different schooling approaches in American education today
    b. no one since the death of John Dewey
    c. an attitude more than by actual classroom practices
    d. all of the above

Answer Key

A. B	2. A	3. C	4. C	5. D
6. A	7. B	8. B	9. C	10. D
11. D	12. C	13. D	14. D	15. A
16. A	17. D	18. B	19. C	20. C
21. A	22. B	23. C	24. C	25. A
26. B	27. A			

Chapter 12

Contemporary School Reform: 1983-1992

CHAPTER OBJECTIVES

Among the objectives that Chapter 12 seeks to achieve are these:

1. Chapter 12 corresponds most directly to Chapter 7 because of historical similarities in the two eras of school reform, but students are intended to understand that several of the chapters in Part I similarly focus on major school reform movements.

2. Students should be able to distinguish between the "first wave" and "second wave" of contemporary school reform and see that our current period exhibits dimensions of both.

3. Students should understand four major themes prominent in the past decade of school reform: a particular definition of educational excellence; a tension among excellence, diversity, and equity; an emerging attention to school choice; and restructuring in school governance and the teaching profession.

4. Students should become familiar with data on the major achievements of the contemporary school reform movement.

5. Students should evaluate the extent to which a critical political economic analysis of current school reform, presented in this chapter, explains available data.

6. Students should assess how well the current school reform movement can be expected to improve educational outcomes in the face of pervasive socioeconomic inequalities.

CHAPTER OVERVIEW

Chapter 12 begins by making explicit something implied throughout Part I of this volume: that one route to understanding American educational history is examining the various reform movements (e.g., common school reform, progressive reform, Cold War-era reform) that have shaped American schooling. Each of these reform movements, of course, may be understood as a response to significantly changing cultural conditions. This chapter's treatment of the contemporary school reform movement corresponds to Chapter 7, which recounts a school reform movement to which our current era is often compared: the Conant era reform following the launching of the Soviet Sputnik. While the social and economic conditions that precipitated the school reform of the 1980s are not so dramatic as the first launching of a human-made satellite, they are nonetheless significant and include: first, the decline of manufacturing as the economic base of the U. S. and the concurrent rise in information processing, service industries, and high technology; second, our declining ability to compete in world markets, leading to the U. S. changing from the world's major lending nation to the world's major debtor nation; third, the apparent decline in the academic skills of American students as compared to past American performance and present performance of students in other industrialized nations; and, fourth, the growing cultural and ethnic diversity of students in American classrooms.

The four major themes that may be said to characterize the last decade of school reform include: first, an academic achievement definition of educational excellence; second, a tension between concerns for excellence and concerns for diversity and equity; third, student and parent choice in schooling; and, fourth, restructuring in school governance, school processes, and the teaching profession. Results of these four major thrusts are examined before turning to a critical view of contemporary school reform.

In this critical view, there appears to be significant evidence that the sources of the nation's economic problems reside primarily in economic and political policies, not in schooling policies. Thus, it is not clear that solutions to our economic woes are likely to be found in school reform efforts, particularly those led by the business community. The chapter also notes that teachers themselves have felt omitted from the national dialogue on school reform. Finally, it would appear that the fundamental social and economic conditions of American society that contribute to poor performance by children in schools (e.g., poverty, unemployment, racism and cultural misunderstanding) are not well addressed by the current school reform movement and are likely to continue to thwart efforts at educational improvement until they are directly addressed by social and economic policies. Another critical perspective on the school reform movement may be found in the Primary Source Reading by Walter Karp, who argues that the school reform movement has not succeeded in educating our nation's youth because it was never intended to.

TEACHING SUGGESTIONS

1. Walter Karp's Primary Source Reading, "Why Johnny Can't Think," can be misused as a simple polemic intended to incite student reactions. However, it is more valuable than that. By drawing upon several school reform documents, the Karp article summarizes a number of significant findings on schooling that preservice teachers can evaluate from their own experience. Karp's attack on schools is a stinging one that rewards careful analysis.

2. A pedagogical move that has been made several times throughout this book has been to question a school reformer's analysis of the problem to be solved as a way of questioning the value of the proposed reform. Orestes Brownson, for example, questions Horace Mann's understanding of democracy itself. Similarly, W. E. B. DuBois questions Booker T. Washington's grasp of the problems of African-Americans in the South. In this chapter, students should be brought to question whether school reformers have adequately understood the basic social and economic problems that undergird the problems of school performance.

ESSAY QUESTIONS

Below are two kinds of essay questions:

    a. short essays or identification questions in which students are asked to write a descriptive paragraph or two to demonstrate their understanding of certain concepts, events, or practices; and

    b. longer essays, which allow students to demonstrate their ability to analyze more complex issues involving several events, concepts, and/or practices.

A. Identify and briefly indicate the significance of an assigned number of the following:

    a. *A Nation at Risk*

    b. *America 2000: An Education Strategy*

    c. "educational excellence"

    d. school choice

    e. school restructuring

    f. contemporary teacher education reform

    g. *Action for Excellence*

    h. Harold Hodgkinson

B. Write a well-ordered essay, 2-3 pages in length, in response to an assigned number of the following questions. Your essay, like the responses required of the questions at the end of each chapter of your text, requires you to take a position on a socio-educational issue and then defend that position with reasoned argument and evidence from the text and from other sources at your disposal. In each essay, you are expected to:

    a. clearly state your position or thesis;

    b. respond to *all parts* of the assigned question;

    c. defend your position with evidence and reasoned argument;

    d. demonstrate college-level writing skills.

1. The current school reform movement has often been compared to the Conant-era reforms following the soviet launching of Sputnik in 1957. To what degree, in your view, are the two reform movements similar and different in political-economic and ideological origins?

2. In your view, which "wave" of contemporary school reform--the first or second wave--seems most successful at achieving its stated or implied goals? Support your position.

3. Clearly summarize and then evaluate Walter Karp's position in "Why Johnny Can't Think." To what degree is Karp's indictment more true for some segments of our school population than for others?

MULTIPLE-CHOICE ITEMS

For each item, select the *best* answer from the four alternatives presented, as supported by your textbook. Students are encouraged to defend answers other than those in the answer key with evidence and argument, which may or may not prove compelling enough to have an alternative answer counted as correct.

1. National defense can be seen as a primary agenda item in which period of school reform?
   a. Progressive Era
   b. post World-War II
   c. Common School era
   d. all of the above

2. The launching of the current school reform movement may reasonably be traced to the publication of
   a. *The American High School Today*
   b. *America 2000*
   c. *A Nation at Risk*
   d. all of the above

3. School reform movements can be analyzed effectively by examining
   a. schooling as a response to new social and economic conditions
   b. the achievement of social consensus on educational values
   c. school restructuring
   d. all of the above

4. One of the underlying causes not usually cited for current school reform is
   a. decline of the industrial base in the U.S.
   b. decline of S.A.T scores
   c. decline of support for school lunch programs
   d. all of the above

5. In the ten years from 1974 to 1984, high-school dropout rates among white students
    a. rose steadily
    b. slowly declined
    c. stayed about the same
    d. all of the above

6. In the same period, high-school completion rates for African American students
    a. increased measurably
    b. decreased steadily
    c. stayed about the same
    d. all of the above

7. The academic subjects identified as most "basic" in *A Nation at Risk* and in *America 2000* are
    a. essentially the same
    b. noticeably different in some respects
    c. not very similar at all
    d. all of the above

8. In *America 2000*, the issue of multiculturalism in education
    a. is strongly emphasized
    b. is nearly overlooked
    c. is omitted entirely
    d. all of the above

9. The Holmes Group and the Carnegie Forum both recommend
    a. restructuring the teaching profession
    b. eliminating college programs of teacher certification
    c. Federal control of teacher certification
    d. all of the above

10. "Restructuring," whether of school governance or curriculum or the teaching profession,
   a. is unique to the current school reform movement and was not found in early movements
   b. is found in one way or another in each of the reform movements discussed throughout this book
   c. has been rejected by most contemporary school reform advocates
   d. all of the above

11. Both the Holmes Group and the Carnegie Forum seek to influence the teaching profession by
   a. establishing more centralized influence over professional preparation and standards
   b. decentralizing control over the profession
   c. allowing schools and colleges of education to set their own standards for teacher certification
   d. all of the above

12. One of the effects of the first wave of school reform seems to be that
   a. teachers' salaries increased
   b. emphasis on vocational education in public schools declined
   c. career ladders were instituted in at least some states
   d. all of the above

13. Frank Margonis's analysis questions the contemporary school reform movement's basic assumption that
   a. school reform can help educate students better
   b. teachers should have a greater voice in school decision making
   c. school inadequacy is largely responsible for the nation's economic decline
   d. all of the above

14. A basic economic factor cited by Margonis as indicative of how the business sector, rather than schools, has contributed to economic decline in the U.S. is

    a. corporate flight from one location to another, including abroad, to obtain the most profitable plant locations

    b. the international economy

    c. escalating corporate income taxes

    d. all of the above

15. Christine Shea's analysis of the concept "learning to learn" in such documents as *Action for Excellence*

    a. endorses the concept because it is consistent with a commitment to critical thinking

    b. criticizes the minimal-competency approach of this orientation

    c. finds this idea to be the strongest part of the early school reform movement

    d. all of the above

16. The emerging service economy in the U.S. provides the kind of employment

    a. that re-trains most blue-collar workers for new industrial skills

    b. that doesn't place high educational demands on most employees

    c. that increases the percentage of college-educated people needed in the workplace

    d. all of the above

17. While the recommendation of *Action for Excellence* that there should be a national plan for educational reform has been heeded

    a. the recommendation that there be such a plan for the economy has not been heeded

    b. it has been rejected by the business community

    c. the plan needs constitutional endorsement by the fifty states

    d. all of the above

18. President Reagan resisted a national plan for education because

    a. it was politically unpopular to support it

    b. he favored a more ideologically conservative laissez-faire approach to schooling that would not require federal assistance to the states

    c. he thought it favored business interests too much

    d. all of the above

19. The current collaboration between business and government in educational reform
    a. is a development for which there is no precedent in the twentieth century
    b. is a return to 19th century classical liberalism
    c. is thoroughly consistent with corporate liberal ideology
    d. all of the above

20. The authors seem to be skeptical of business-education partnerships because
    a. the top-down decision-making characteristic of business organization may not be a desirable model for schooling in a democratic culture
    b. such partnerships assume that the goals of education should be determined in large part by the needs of the business community
    c. the measure of success in business is profit, which may conflict with the measures of success in education that emphasis human development
    d. all of the above

21. The authors note that the Bush administration's support for schools of choice
    a. was undermined by the administration's support for centrally prescribed educational goals
    b. is a clear movement in a positive educational direction
    c. never became articulated in any official documents
    d. all of the above

22. Stan Karp contends that the willingness of the federal government to fund the school reforms of *America 2000* during the Bush administration
    a. was grossly inadequate to the task of bringing about those reforms
    b. was the central source of power that would actually achieve those reforms
    c. helped Bush live up to his claim to be "the education President"
    d. all of the above

23. The voices of teachers in the contemporary school reform movement
    a. have been instrumental in shaping both the first and second waves of reform
    b. have been virtually ignored since the beginning
    c. have not influenced, but have at least strongly supported, the progress of reform
    d. all of the above

24. The authors appear to take the position that
    a. the contemporary school reform movement has the capacity to address the basic causes of school failure in the U.S.
    b. fundamental economic problems need to be addressed directly at their source through economic means rather than indirectly through educational means
    c. the contemporary school reform movement is sufficiently independent of business control that it successfully puts the interests of children first
    d. all of the above

25. Researchers Stan Karp and Christine Shea appear to agree that
    a. the contemporary school reform movement was never designed to benefit all children in U.S. schools
    b. school reform in the U.S. is hopeless
    c. with some minor adjustments, the current school reform movement is likely to succeed in restructuring schools for the benefit of nearly all children
    d. all of the above

Answer Key

1. B	2. C	3. A	4. C	5. C
6. A	7. B	8. B	9. A	10. B
11. A	12. D	13. C	14. B	15. B
16. B	17. A	18. B	19. C	20. D
21. A	22. A	23. A	24. B	25. A

Chapter 13

Conclusion: School and Contemporary Society

CHAPTER OBJECTIVES

Among the objectives that Chapter 13 seeks to achieve are these:

1. The purpose of this chapter is in part to remind preservice teachers of why they need to have the best understandings possible of the political economic and ideological dimensions of the social context of schooling. A primary reason is that these dimensions are fundamental aspects of the problems that teachers face moment by moment in their classrooms.

2. Students should review some of the political economic and ideological conditions that constitute significant obstacles to equal school success for students from all social groups.

3. Students should see that the primary ideological condition in society today is not an issue of conservative or liberal, Republican or Democrat, but the dominant ideology of corporate liberalism that pervades mainstream political and educational thought.

4. Students should recognize that a part of that dominant ideology is committed to solving pervasive social and economic problems through schooling, an intention that makes promises for teachers they are not likely to be able to keep. This chapter tries to refocus prospective teachers on educational goals that they can realistically achieve for all of their students, regardless of cultural background.

CHAPTER OVERVIEW

Chapter 13 is a brief discussion that picks up where Chapter 12 left off. One primary purpose of this chapter is to review some of the more salient contemporary social conditions that form the context of teaching and learning in schools in the 1990s. These social conditions, which include gross economic inequality, extraordinarily high numbers of people murdered and imprisoned, and other social pathologies, can be paralyzing for prospective teachers who hope that their teaching will one day make a difference in the lives of students whose environments are hostile to their development. However, this chapter argues that teachers can, in fact, make a significant difference in the lives of their students if teachers understand the obstacles that confront them. By focusing on the qualities that each of their students needs to develop to live a fulfilling life as a worker, a citizen, and a person, prospective teachers can formulate goals and devise classroom strategies that will open doors for students for whom such doors might not otherwise be open. It is the position of this concluding chapter that teachers can confront the more grim realities of the social context of schooling without losing hope for their students and for themselves as educators. An important part of sustaining a realistic hope is learning to distinguish between educational promises they can keep and educational promises that they cannot keep. This chapter, like this entire volume, suggests that teachers should be wary of making promises that their teaching will correct social and economic problems that did not originate with the schools. A promise that teachers can keep, however, is that, given the necessary resources, they can teach children from all ethnic and economic backgrounds to learn to read, write, compute, and think well. As evidence for this view, we conclude the volume with a Primary Source Reading written by a veteran teacher and principal who is currently succeeding in her efforts to educate students of diverse backgrounds at the Central Park East schools in New York City.

TEACHING SUGGESTIONS

1. The Primary Source Reading by Deborah Meier is another opportunity for prospective teachers to evaluate whether the critical idealism of this volume can be found in practice in schools today. Meier's article is based on her own successes with students from a wide diversity of backgrounds and offers preservice teachers a chance to assess what components of her schools make these schools so successful.

2. Of particular interest in the Meier reading is her identification of five qualities she would like to find in prospective teachers. Preservice teachers are known to be concerned about their own qualities and capacity to teach well. The five qualities Meier identifies are useful as criteria in two ways. First, prospective teachers can assess whether they themselves "measure up" well to these five; and, second, they can evaluate whether and how these five criteria address the problems of schooling that tend to occur when students from diverse cultural backgrounds enter middle-class American schools.

3. This chapter suggests an overarching justification for school teachers' need to understand the social foundations of education: that the problems that teachers face moment by moment in their classrooms have dimensions that are sociological, historical, economic, ideological, and so on, and that schooling problems are not adequately understood unless those social dimensions of the problems are recognized. Students and faculty can test these hypotheses together by identifying examples of typical problems faced by teachers and then identifying what social foundations of those problems might be important for teachers to understand.

ESSAY QUESTIONS

Below are two kinds of essay questions:

   a. short essays or identification questions in which students are asked to write a descriptive paragraph or two to demonstrate their understanding of certain concepts, events, or practices; and

   b. longer essays, which allow students to demonstrate their ability to analyze more complex issues involving several events, concepts, and/or practices.

A. Identify and briefly indicate the significance of an assigned number of the following:
   a. two-wage-earner families
   b. *We're Number One*
   c. increasing ethnic and linguistic diversity in the U.S.
   d. educational remedies for economic problems
   e. U.S. voter participation

    f. the conservative political-economic agenda of the 1980s:

    g. Deborah Meier

    h. Central Park East Schools

B. Write a well-ordered essay, 2-3 pages in length, in response to an assigned number of the following questions. Your essay, like the responses required of the questions at the end of each chapter of your text, requires you to take a position on a socio-educational issue and then defend that position with reasoned argument and evidence from the text and from other sources at your disposal. In each essay, you are expected to:

    a. clearly state your position or thesis;

    b. respond to *all parts* of the assigned question;

    c. defend your position with evidence and reasoned argument;

    d. demonstrate college-level writing skills.

1. Evaluate the following assessment: Chapter 13 is fundamentally pessimistic about the chances that schooling can make much difference at all in people's lives. Defend your evaluation with evidence from the text, and explain the degree to which you agree with the authors' position, as you have identified it.

2. The authors evidently intend the Deborah Meier selection to show that admirable educational achievements in contemporary society are possible, and that there is much to be learned from the examples of success. How well does the selection achieve the author's intent?

3. It might be said that the Central Park Schools educate their teachers as well as their students. Elaborate on that claim and evaluate whether public schools in general can be expected to become such educational places for teachers and students.

MULTIPLE-CHOICE ITEMS

For each item, select the *best* answer from the four alternatives presented, as supported by your textbook. Students are encouraged to defend answers other than those in the answer key with evidence and argument, which may or may not prove compelling enough to have an alternative answer counted as correct.

1. It is the position of this chapter that teachers have
    a. virtually no voice in making important decisions that affect their work lives
    b. significant voice in making important professional decisions and therefore require understanding of the schools' social contexts
    c. little desire to be engaged in educational policy decisions
    d. all of the above

2. The authors imply that teachers need to understand economic conditions in the U.S. in part because
    a. children's learning can be affected by conditions of poverty
    b. such understanding is part of a good liberal arts education
    c. then teachers can fight structured economic inequality
    d. all of the above

3. The authors cite the lamentable data from Shapiro's *We're Number One* to illustrate that
    a. schools cannot do much for children in such tragic socio-economic circumstances
    b. teachers need to understand the forces acting negatively on children if they are to counter them effectively in the classroom
    c. teachers are in a good position to change the social structure
    d. all of the above

4. Among the promises that teachers *can* keep is the promise that
    a. improved education in the nation's schools will lead directly to national economic success
    b. schools can correct most social problems, even if they did not originate in the schools
    c. schools can help children from all socio-economic and ethnic backgrounds to achieve academic success
    d. all of the above

5. Today's corporate liberalism is
   a. characteristic of the "right" but not the "left"
   b. directly opposed to today's conservativism
   c. a general area of political consensus that encompasses the views of liberals and conservatives, republicans and democrats
   d. all of the above

6. The 1980s were a time of strong economic gain for
   a. those in the upper income brackets
   b. the middle class
   c. nearly everyone across the income spectrum
   d. all of the above

7. It is the view of the authors that answering the question "What does it mean to lead a good and fulfilling life?" is
   a. the responsibility of teachers and policy makers
   b. an idealistic but irrelevant question, when the power of ideological hegemony is recognized
   c. a question that each student in schools can be helped to answer for him- or herself
   d. all of the above

8. One of the five qualities that Deborah Meier does not list among the desired qualities of a prospective teacher is
   a. academic excellence
   b. good classroom management skills
   c. well-developed skills in lesson-planning
   d. all of the above

9. Meier takes the following position on school choice:
   a. she opposes it for most schools, but not for CPSS
   b. she believes it should be the policy for all schools
   c. she doesn't think it is essential to school success
   d. all of the above

10. The authors believe the "four freedoms" Deborah Meier identifies as important to her schools' successes are
    a. not attainable by most schools, thereby limiting the generalizability of CPSS successes to other schools
    b. freedoms that other schools can and should attain
    c. a recipe for teacher "burnout"
    d. all of the above

Answer Key

1. B	2. A	3. B	4. C	5. C
6. A	7. C	8. D	9. B	10. B

USER SURVEY

SCHOOL AND SOCIETY: EDUCATIONAL PRACTICE AS SOCIAL EXPRESSION

Name _____   Dept _____

School _____   City/State _____

Phone _____   Office Hrs _____

PART ONE: COURSE INFORMATION

1. The course in which I use *School and Society* has the following title and characteristics.

   Course title: _____

   Course length: ___1 qrt ___2 qrts ___2 sem ___2 sem

   Course level (check all that apply): ___fresh ___soph ___ jr ___ sr ___ grad

   Course is ___ required ___elective
   and is taken by: ___elem majors ___ sec majors ___ spec ed majors
   other _____

   Annual enrollment (all sections): ___ under 50 ___ 50-100 ___ 100-200
   ___ over 200

   Prerequisite courses: _____
   _____

   Do students in this course have a prior or concurrent practicum experience?
   ___ yes ___ no

      Nature of practicum experience (check all that apply).
      ___ class observation ___ interviewing ___ teacher assistant ___ tutoring
      other _____

   What text did this one replace? _____

   What text(s), if any, are you using in addition to this one? _____
   _____

   My own professional training is primarily in the field of

   _____ Social Foundations of Education
   _____ Philosophy or History of Education
   _____ Curriculum & Instruction
       Other (please) specify_____

CUT ALONG THIS LINE

PART TWO: TEXT FEATURES

Please take a moment to react to each of the following statements about the book's key features.

2. I would the two-part book plan, which integrates historical perspectives on important educational issues (Part I) with contemporary perspectives on those same issues (Part II).
___ yes ___ no

Suggestions for improvement.

3. I like the three-part (political economy-ideology-school practice) framework that is used to analyze educational issues and practices. ___ yes ___ no

Suggestions for improvement.

4. I like the end-of-chapter readings, which offer personal positions regarding important chapter content and, together with the discussion questions, provide students with an opportunity to develop their critical thinking skills.

Suggestions for improvement.

5. I like the heavy diversity/equity focus found in chapters 4, 6, 9 and 10.
___ yes ___ no

Suggestions for improvement.

PART THREE: CHAPTER RATINGS

A table of contents follows. On a scale of 1 to 10 (**10 being highest quality and most useful**) please rate both the quality of each chapter and that chapter's usefulness in your course. Use the space provided to make any suggestions for improvement that come to mind. If additional space is needed, please use the back of the page to complete your answer.

Quality	Useful	Chapter
_____	_____	1. Understanding School and Society
_____	_____	2. Liberty and Literacy: The Jeffersonian Ideal
_____	_____	3. School as Public Institution: The Common School Era
_____	_____	4. Schooling and Social Inequality: The Booker T. Washington Solution

_____ _____   5.   Education for the Vocations: The Progressive Era

_____ _____   6.   Culture and Control: Schooling and the American Indian

_____ _____   7.   National School Reform: The Cold War Era

_____ _____   8.   Literacy and Liberty in the United States Today

_____ _____   9.   Public School Teaching: A Gendered Profession

_____ _____   10. Schooling and Social Inequality: Race, Gender, and Class

_____ _____   11. Vocational and Liberal Education Today

_____ _____   12. Contemporary School Reform: 1983-1992

_____ _____   13. Conclusion: School and Contemporary Society

PART IV: STRENGTHS, WEAKNESSES, AND RECOMMENDATIONS

6. What do you consider the book's two greatest strengths?

7. What do you consider the book's two greatest weaknesses?

8. Please indicate any changes not already covered that you feel would strengthen the book.

Many thanks for your help. Please return the completed questionnaire along with a copy of your course syllabus to:

Lane Akers
70 Smith Street
Chappaqua, NY   10514